Try the spirits

Try the spirits

Volume 1

Was C S Lewis truly 'Our greatest Christian writer'?

Philip Yancey—'turning the grace of God into lasciviousness'?

Alpha—Attend or Avoid?

Cecil Andrews

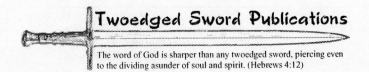

Twoedged Sword Publications

The word of God is sharper than any twoedged sword, piercing even to the dividing asunder of soul and spirit. (Hebrews 4:12)

© Cecil Andrews 2004

First published 2004

ISBN 0-9547205-2-0

Twoedged Sword Publications
PO Box 266, Waterlooville, PO7 5ZT
www.twoedgedswordpublications.co.uk

Preface

When I first formed 'Take Heed' Ministries some fourteen years ago most of the warnings issued on spiritual deception would have referred to matters outside of professing Christendom. Today the spiritual make-up of that professing Christendom is both very different and very dangerous. There has been a Biblically-predicted (1 Timothy 4:1 and 2 Timothy 4:3) marked decline in discernment amongst professing Christians and the result is that the questionable views of certain apologists, authors and advocates, who are viewed by many as Christian, have increased dramatically both in popularity and influence. This book is an attempt to bring Biblical truth to bear on three such current dangers that are deceiving many. May the One who is 'truth' (John 14:6) be pleased to use it for the cause of His truth and His glory alone.

Cecil Andrews
'Take Heed' Ministries
20 September 2004

Contents

Was C S Lewis truly 'Our greatest Christian writer'?

Introduction

Since early 2002, local Northern Ireland Pastor of ChristChurch, Belfast, and well-known writer, Derick Bingham has been engaged in what seems like a determined, personal crusade to promote the stories and writings of C S Lewis. In his *Thought For The Weekend* published in the *Belfast Telegraph* of 5 January 2002, Derick Bingham wrote:

'It is now the evening of September 19th, 1931 and an Ulsterman called C S Lewis has just had some guests to dinner... One of the guests J R R Tolkien is a Professor of Anglo Saxon and shares with Lewis a deep love of the books of George McDonald, a Scottish Presbyterian minister of the 19th century who wrote thirty novels in his time. As a sixteen-year-old atheist, Lewis had come across the writing of Mr McDonald and heard for the first time, he later admitted, the voice of Holiness. He also famously stated "*a young atheist cannot guard his faith too carefully*" and stated that he had not been searching for God any more than a mouse goes searching for a cat. But Lewis had been "searched" and had quite recently admitted that God was God, but he was categorically not a Christian believer... Lewis could not see the relevance of Christian truths similar to those found in pagan mythologies – for instance the ideas of sacrifice, propitiation, the shedding of blood, communion and redemption. Tolkien maintained that the difference between the Christian story and other stories was that it came from a God who was real and from a God whose dying could transform those who believed in him... Three days later, while sitting in the sidecar of his brother's motorcycle on the way to Whipsnade Zoo, C S Lewis was converted to Christ. "When I set out I did not believe that Jesus Christ is the Son of God. And when I reached the zoo, I did" he wrote in his book *Surprised by Joy*.'

At this point I want to make three comments about what Derick Bingham wrote.

1. He has stated that C S Lewis was an atheist who came to the view that 'God was God' – but this did not equal being a Christian. [At this point Lewis would be viewed as a 'theist'.]

2. On the evening in question, C S Lewis listened to the views of J R R Tolkien who was a Roman Catholic. Derick Bingham has stated that Lewis 'could not see the relevance of Christian truths... for instance the ideas of sacrifice, propitiation, the shedding of blood, communion and redemption'. Any explanation of these 'Christian truths' that might have been given to Lewis by Tolkien would have been the unscriptural, erroneous Roman Catholic understanding of these 'truths'.

3. Derick Bingham concludes that the declaration by Lewis that 'Jesus Christ is the Son of God' is sufficient evidence of the progression of Lewis from 'theist' to 'Christian convert'.

In relation to J R R Tolkien and his Roman Catholicism let me quote the following extracts from his biography as found on the Tolkien Society Web site <http://www.tolkiensociety.org>.

'Certainly his father, Arthur Reuel Tolkien, considered himself nothing if not English. Arthur was a bank clerk and went to South Africa in the 1890s for better prospects of promotion. There he was joined by his bride, Mabel Suffield... so John ("Ronald" to family and early friends) was born in Bloemfontein SA on 3 January 1892... on 15 February 1896 his father died, and he, his mother and his younger brother Hilary returned to England, or more particularly, the West Midlands... Then they moved to the somewhat more pleasant Birmingham suburb of Edgbaston. *However in the meantime, something of profound significance has occurred which estranged Mabel and her children from both sides of the family: in 1900 together with her sister May, she was received into the Roman Catholic Church. From then on both Ronald and Hilary were brought up in the faith of Pio Nono and remained devout Catholics throughout their lives.* The parish priest who visited the family regularly was the half-Spanish half-Welsh Father Francis Morgan... He [Tolkien] soon became one of the founder members of a loose grouping of Oxford friends with similar interests known as "The Inklings"... Other prominent members included... Dyson... and *above all C S Lewis who became one of Tolkien's closest friends, and for whose return to Christianity, Tolkien was at least partly responsible...* On 27 November 1971 Edith [Tolkien's wife] died and Ronald soon returned to Oxford, to rooms provided by Merton College. Ronald died on 2 September 1973. *He and Edith are buried together in a single grave in the Catholic section of Wolvercote cemetery* in the northern suburbs of Oxford.'

The evidence is clear that Tolkien was committed to Roman Catholicism which, as God's people know, often to their cost, is no friend of Biblical, evangelical Christianity and it is extremely disturbing to see Derick Bingham viewing both Tolkien and his religion as being Christian – in his booklet *Walking With Giants* Derick Bingham wrote:

'Now in the twenty first century the books and films of the books of Lewis and Tolkien fascinate

11

millions of people around the earth. At the heart
of that friendship, though, lay the importance of
the person of Jesus Christ. *The Lord of THESE*
[emphasis mine] *giants of literature is of course
as real today as ever.'*

In the closing line of his *Thought For The Weekend* published in
the *Belfast Telegraph* of 5 January 2002, Derick Bingham wrote:

'Tolkien and Lewis still speak. And how!'

Derick Bingham refers to these men as 'giants' – drawing on the
lessons we learn from the story of another giant, named Goliath,
I would urge God's people to 'TAKE HEED'.

As a footnote to Derick Bingham's *Thought For The Weekend*
published in the *Belfast Telegraph* of 14 September 2002, there
was this statement:

'For those interested, Derick Bingham's free
booklet on the story of the conversion to faith of
C S Lewis, particularly through a conversation
with J R R Tolkien, entitled *Walking with Giants*
is available by writing to...'

I wrote away for a copy of this booklet and shall be commenting
upon its contents shortly, but to further illustrate this crusade to
promote the story of C S Lewis let me now quote from the latter
portion of Derick Bingham's *Thought For The Weekend*
published in the *Belfast Telegraph* of 12 October 2002:

'I leave his [the Apostle Paul's] words with you
to consider over this weekend. I shall, God
willing, be high in the Swiss Alps by the time you
read them, expounding an Ulsterman's view of
the Gospel at a special weekend, namely the
views of C S Lewis.'

The final promotion of Lewis by Derick Bingham that I want to
refer to is the article that was published in the *Lifetimes*
magazine of October 2002. This article by Derick Bingham took
the form of a review of a book called *Jack; a life of C S Lewis*
by George Sayer. In his article Derick Bingham wrote:

'For me the chapter entitled *The Pilgrim's Progress* gives most helpful information on the conversion of C S Lewis on September 22nd 1931 while sitting in the sidecar of his brother's motorcycle en route to Whipsnade Zoo!... It is wonderful to at last see people in Northern Ireland beginning to recognize Lewis for the spiritual giant he was... Lewis, *our greatest Christian writer* [emphasis mine] is now the best selling Christian author in all of history.'

Again, as a footnote to this article, the following information was published:

'Derick Bingham is a teaching pastor with ChristChurch, Belfast. This month, DV, he will hold a seminar at Villars in Switzerland on C S Lewis and will give an address at the 75th anniversary of the N I Civil Service Christian Union in the Great Hall, Parliament Buildings, Stormont to a specially invited audience of politicians and civil servants on the subject of the conversion of C S Lewis.'

In the light of the foregoing I hope you will agree that I was certainly not exaggerating when I referred to 'a determined, personal crusade' by Derick Bingham to promote C S Lewis.

I mentioned earlier that I would refer to the booklet on Lewis by Derick Bingham called *Walking with Giants* and in it Derick Bingham again refers to the time in 1929 when the then atheist, Lewis, finally came to the view that 'God was God'. Derick Bingham wrote:

'Lewis now believed in God. He was a theist, that is, he believed in the creation of the universe by one God but he was not yet a Christian.'

However, on the preceding page Derick Bingham quotes more extensively from what Lewis wrote about this 1929 transformation. Lewis wrote:

'That which I had greatly feared had come upon me... I gave in and admitted that God was God and knelt and prayed: perhaps that night *the most dejected and reluctant convert in all England...* but who can duly adore that love which will open the high gates to a prodigal who is brought in kicking, struggling, resentful and darting his eyes in every direction for a chance to escape?'

I have read other reports (for example by Dr Bruce L Edwards) that chart the 'progression' of Lewis as being from atheist-to-theist-to-Christian but the terminology used by Lewis in 1929 seems to me to be more than that of a 'mere theist'. I just wonder has Derick Bingham sought to fully think through and explain what spiritual reality Lewis was seeking to convey when he referred to himself as a 'convert' who 'knelt and prayed', as a 'prodigal' and as one 'brought in'? Is there any evidence that Lewis himself drew such a clear distinction between his 'conversion' in 1929 [to that of 'theist'] and his 'conversion' in 1931 [to that of 'Christian']? Perhaps there is such evidence available and if so it would be very helpful if Derick Bingham were to put it in the public domain.

Referring again to the night of the conversation between Lewis and Tolkien, in his booklet Derick Bingham also stated this:

'Tolkien went home and Hugo Dyson, another friend and academic, continued to talk with Lewis... He emphasised that the one who believes in Christ receives peace and forgiveness of sins.'

Three days later Lewis declared that he believed that 'Jesus Christ is the Son of God'. Perhaps I'm ultra cautious but I am very hesitant to simply accept that someone who declares that 'God is God' and that 'Jesus Christ is the Son of God' can automatically be considered to be a genuine Christian convert. Mormons can easily declare that 'God is God' and that 'Jesus Christ is the Son of God' It is one thing to 'believe IN Christ' but quite another matter to 'believe ON Christ' – that is, the 'Christ' revealed in the Bible.

In my Bible I read of a man with 'an unclean spirit' and he said to Christ 'I know thee who thou art, the Holy One of God' (Mark 1:23-24). When Christ came to 'the country of the Gergesenes, there met him two possessed with devils... And behold they cried out, what have we to do with thee, Jesus, thou Son of God' (Matthew 8:28-29). Then in James 2:19 I read 'Thou believest that there is one God; thou doest well: the devils also believe and tremble'. It is clear from scripture that to believe that 'God is God' and that 'Jesus Christ is the Son of God' is not a sure testimony to possessing God's 'so great salvation' (Hebrews 2:3).

In my Bible I read the following 'Whosoever transgresseth and abideth not in the doctrine of Christ, hath not God. He that abideth in the doctrine of Christ, he hath both the Father and the Son' (2 John 1:9). A true Christian convert will not only be right about the *person* of Christ but he will also be right about the *work* of Christ. This is the divine revelation given to those who savingly *'believe ON Christ'* – listen to Christ in Matthew 11:25 'I thank thee O father, Lord of heaven and earth, because thou hast hid these things from the wise and prudent and hast revealed them unto babes'. In the great chapter where Christ speaks of being 'born again' we subsequently read in John 3:27 where John the Baptist said concerning spiritual knowledge 'A man can receive nothing except it be given him from heaven'.

I often hear the expression 'A person is not justified [acquitted by God] by their words' and that is true but 'the words of a person' will testify that they have been truly 'justified'. The words of a 'justified person' will show that they are 'abiding in the doctrine of Christ' and that they truly 'have both the Father and the Son' (2 John 1:9).

To test if someone is truly a genuine Christine convert who is 'abiding in the doctrine of Christ' it is scripturally legitimate to examine what all those professing to be Christian say and write publicly for we read in 1 John 4:1 'Beloved, believe not every spirit, but try [test] the spirits whether they are of God: because many false prophets are gone out into the world'. In the Berean spirit, commended by Paul in Acts 17:11, I want now to consider some of the publicly expressed views of C S Lewis to see if he truly merits Derick Bingham's appellation that he is 'our greatest Christian writer'.

Prior to even considering compiling any report, most of the concerns that I held concerning the writings of C S Lewis were based upon reports compiled by other concerned Christian apologists (some of which I will refer to later). However, recently I have taken time to look at what Lewis wrote in his book *Mere Christianity* and I have been so shocked by what I have read that I was simply compelled to write this report, particularly in the light of all the high-profile promotion being given to Lewis by Derick Bingham.

The teachings of C S Lewis on Repentance

In his 2001 report entitled *C S Lewis and Evangelicals Today*, David Cloud of *Way of Life Literature*, wrote:

> 'The late British author C S Lewis [1898-1963] is extremely popular with Evangelicals today. According to a *Christianity Today* reader's poll in 1998, Lewis was rated the most influential writer. Though Lewis died in 1963, sales of his books have risen to two million a year. In an article commemorating the 100th anniversary of Lewis's birth, J I Packer called him our "patron saint".'

In the light of the many endorsements given last year by local Pastor and well-known writer, Derick Bingham [as detailed by myself in the New Year 2003 *News From The Front*], I have no doubt that local sales of Lewis's writings may well have been substantially boosted. In my Introduction I wrote:

> '...recently I have taken time to look at what Lewis wrote in his book *Mere Christianity* and I have been so shocked by what I have read that I was simply compelled to write this report, particularly in the light of all the high-profile promotion being given to Lewis by Derick Bingham.'

Let us examine what Mr Lewis had to say in a number of crucial doctrinal areas. The first doctrine that I wish to consider is that of *repentance*. The first command of the Lord as recorded in Mark's gospel is 'Repent and believe the gospel' (Mark 1:15). Then, in the midst of his sermon on Mars Hill in Athens, the Apostle Paul declared to the philosophers gathered around him 'And the times of this ignorance God overlooked, but now commandeth all men everywhere to repent' (Acts 17:30). In the first five verses of Luke 13 the Lord Himself twice issued this warning to his listeners 'Except ye repent ye shall all likewise perish'.

It is clear that repentance is no 'soft option' and so a correct understanding of it is absolutely vital to the eternal well being of every individual. In Vine's *Expository Dictionary of Old and New Testament Words* we read the following on page 525 under 'Repent, Repentance':

> 'Signifies "to change one's mind or purpose," always in the NT involving a *change* for the better, *an amendment*, and always, except Luke 17:3-4, of "repentance" *from sin*... In the NT the subject chiefly has reference to "repentance" from sin and this change of mind involves both *a turning from sin* and *a turning to God*. The parable of the Prodigal Son is an outstanding illustration of this.'

In one of my daily devotional books, *Footprints of Faith* edited by Alan Cairns, the meditation for 21 March ends with the following quotation:

> 'Repentance is the relinquishment of any practice from the conviction that it has offended God.'
> (Joseph Addison)

I think that quote captures well the essence of Biblical repentance.

From God's Word we also learn that repentance is a gracious gift to undeserving sinners held in Satan's grip. Paul wrote in 2 Timothy 2:24-26 'And the servant of the Lord must not strive, but be gentle unto all men, apt to teach, patient. In meekness instructing those that oppose him, if God perhaps will give them repentance to the acknowledging of the truth, And that they may recover themselves out of the snare of the devil, who are taken captive by him at his will.'

Commenting on these verses Matthew Henry wrote:

> '*Repentance is God's gift...* The same God who gives us the discovery of the truth *does by His grace bring us to the acknowledging of it*, otherwise our hearts would continue in rebellion against it... When sinners repent, *those who before were led captive by the devil at his will* come to be led into the glorious liberty of the children of God and have their wills melted into the will of the Lord Jesus.'

On page 1878 of his *Study Bible* notes, Pastor John MacArthur wrote:

> 'All true repentance is produced by God's sovereign grace [Ephesians 2:7]... When God, by grace, grants saving faith it includes the granting of repentance from sin. Neither is it a human work.'

The book *Mere Christianity* written by C S Lewis is divided into three 'books' and chapter four of Book Two is entitled *The Perfect Penitent*. I want to quote some extracts from this chapter (pages 53-58) to help you understand how C S Lewis understood and articulated his view of repentance. Referring to the Lord Jesus, C S Lewis wrote:

> 'What did He come to do? Well, to teach of course; but as soon as you look into the New Testament or any other Christian writing you will find they are constantly talking about something different – about His death and His coming to life again. It is obvious that Christians think the chief point of the story lies there. They think the main thing He came to earth to do was to suffer and be

killed.' [Paul under inspiration taught this – see I Timothy 1:15; 1 Corinthians 15:1-4; Galatians 6:14 as did the Lord in Matthew 16:21; 17:22-23; 20:28]. C S Lewis continues 'Christ volunteered to be punished instead and so God let us off. Now I admit that even this theory does not seem to me quite so immoral and so silly as it used to be; but that is not the point I want to make. What I came to see later on was that neither this theory nor any other is Christianity... Theories about Christ's death are not Christianity.'

In 1 Corinthians 15:1-4, referred to above, Paul sets out in the clearest of terms what constitutes 'the Gospel' – it is not a 'theory' – it is a declaration of the historical reality of the death, burial and resurrection ('according to the scriptures') of the Lord Jesus Christ. If 'the Gospel' is not 'Christianity' then why would the Lord Himself instruct His followers to 'Go ye into all the world and preach the gospel to every creature' (Mark 16:15) and why would Paul believe that he would actually be failing in his calling to be an Apostle by declaring 'Woe is unto me, if I preach not the gospel' (1 Corinthians 9:16)?

C S Lewis continues:

'We are told that Christ was killed for us, that His death has washed out our sins and that by dying He disabled death itself. That is the formula. That is Christianity. That is what has to be believed... Now on the face of it that is a very silly theory... On the other hand, if you think of a debt, there is plenty of point in a person who has some assets paying it on behalf of someone who has not... when one person has got himself into a hole, the trouble of getting him out usually falls on a kind friend. Now what was the sort of "hole" man had got himself into? He had tried to set up on his own... he is a rebel who must lay down his arms. Laying down your arms, surrendering, saying you are sorry, realising that you have been on the wrong track… that is the only way out of our "hole." This process of surrender – this movement full speed astern – is what Christians call *repentance*. Now *repentance* is no fun at all. It is something much harder than eating humble pie. It means unlearning all the self-conceit and self-will that we have been training ourselves into for thousands of years. It means killing part of yourself, undergoing a kind of death.'

Perhaps you're thinking to yourself that this all sounds more or less in harmony with what God's Word teaches. Well listen to what C S Lewis goes on to say:

'In fact, it needs a good man to repent. And here comes the catch. Only a bad person needs to repent [true]: only a good person can repent perfectly [false]. The worse you are the more you need it [true] and the less you can do it [not true as it is God's gracious gift – Jeremiah prayed "Ah, Lord God… there is nothing too hard for thee" and God responded "I am the Lord, the God of all flesh; is there anything too hard for me?" (32:17, 27)] …The only person who could do it [repent] perfectly would be a perfect person – and he would not need it. Remember, this repentance, this willing submission to humiliation and a kind of death, is not something God demands of you before He will take you back [not true – look again at the scriptural imperatives quoted earlier] …He could let you off if He chose: it is simply a description of what going back to Him is like.'

What a poisonous mix of truth and error these writings of Mr Lewis are.

C S Lewis continues:

'…we now need God's help in order to do something which God, in His own nature, never does at all – to surrender, to suffer, to submit, to die... But supposing God became a man – suppose our human nature which can suffer and die was amalgamated with God's nature in one person – then that person could help us. He could surrender His will, and suffer and die, because He was man; and He could do it [repent!] perfectly because He was God. You and I can go through this process [repentance] only if God does it in us [true]; but God can do it only if He becomes a man [not true – we read of people in the Old testament like David and Manasseh repenting and that was before Christ's incarnation]. Our attempts at this dying [our repentance] will succeed only if we men share in God's dying [God's repentance!] ...we cannot share God's dying unless God dies; and He cannot die except by being a man [normally true – but remember Mr Lewis is here speaking in terms of "repentance" and not of Christ dying "sacrificially"] ...That is the sense in which He pays our debt and suffers for us what He himself need not suffer at all.'

Back in 1994 I had a series of written exchanges with a strong supporter of the beliefs of Edward Cooney (his followers are often referred to as 'Cooneyites'). In one letter she wrote:

'Believing in a doctrine or doctrines about Jesus is not salvation... With regard to the doctrine of the Atonement... it was *the sacrificial life* of Christ, poured out unto death, even death on the cross, *in perfect obedience* to the will of God. It is by this complete sacrifice of his life that we are reconciled to God... I believe the penal substitution theory [Christ atoningly suffering as a substitute for His people on the Cross] is false doctrine.'

I just wonder was C S Lewis, whilst living in Northern Ireland, ever exposed to Cooneyite teaching as I see echoes of their beliefs in his expressed views. Let me just remind everyone reading this that I am quoting from a chapter of C S Lewis's book *Mere Christianity* and the chapter in question is called *The Perfect Penitent* and clearly from what he has written this is how C S Lewis views Christ. My reading of all this is that Mr Lewis has equated the sinless Lord's innate ability to resist sin with fallen man's necessity to repent of sin. In so doing I believe that Mr Lewis has maligned the impeccable character of our Lord every bit as much as when Kenneth Copeland teaches that the Lord was 'born again' in hell. It seems to me that Mr Lewis has heretically confused the Lord's 'resistance' to sin with 'repentance' from sin – and this is the man that Derick Bingham has hailed as 'our greatest Christian writer'. If anyone would like an audiotape of an excellent sermon on repentance preached by Trevor Watson of Banbridge Baptist Church it may be ordered from me (cost including p&p £2.00).

In his *Dictionary of Theological Terms*, Alan Cairns wrote this definition on page 426:

'Vicarious repentance theory of the Atonement

Also known as the Theory of Sympathy and Identification. We may summarise it under the following points.

1. The only atonement necessary for sin is a perfect repentance.

2. Such a repentance from man would have been sufficient for salvation, had he been able to offer it.

3. Christ offered a perfect repentance on behalf of man and so procured forgiveness.

4. The death of Christ was merely a sympathetic entering into the Father's condemnation of sin, and as such showed the wickedness of sin and condemned it.

The theory is objectionable on various grounds

1. It fails to see that sin makes the sinner liable to punishment.

2. It denies any objective quality in the atonement [i.e. It denies that Christ's atoning death actually and effectively accomplished salvation for anyone].

3. It is a contradiction in terms – repentance is purely a subjective [relates to self] thing and cannot be valid unless it is personal. That Christ felt and sorrowed over the sins He vicariously bore for His people is certain [Psalm 40:12] but it was impossible for Him to turn *back* to God [during His life on earth] from committed sin, for – even in bearing our sins [on the cross] – He had never turned *away* from Him.

4. THERE IS NOT A FRAGMENT OF SCRIPTURAL SUPPORT FOR IT.'

This definition by Mr Cairns seems to perfectly encapsulate the conclusions that I had come to when analysing what Mr Lewis had written on this subject of 'repentance' and it has come as an encouraging confirmation to my own understanding to discover that what I had unearthed had already been identified and quantified by Mr Cairns, who for 33 years has been a lecturer in Systematic Theology in the Theological Hall of the Free Presbyterian Church.

The teachings of C S Lewis on Regeneration

To begin with I want to consider two things: firstly, what is 'regeneration' and secondly, does sinful man have any input into his own 'regeneration'?

In answer to the first question – what is 'regeneration'? let me quote from Vines' *Expository Dictionary of Old and New Testament Words*. On pages 517-518 under the heading 'Regeneration' we read the following:

> *'Palingenesia* "new birth" (*palin* – "again"; *genesis* – "birth") is used of "spiritual regeneration" [Titus 3:5] involving the communication of a *new life*, the two operating powers to produce which are "The Word of Truth" [James 1:18; 1 Peter 1:23] and "The Holy Spirit" [John 3:5-6]... The *new birth* and *regeneration* do not represent successive stages in spiritual experience, they refer to the same event but view it in different aspects. The *new birth* stresses the communication of spiritual life in contrast to the antecedent spiritual death [see Ephesians 2:1]; *regeneration* stresses the inception of a new state of things in contrast with the old' [see 2 Corinthians 5:17].

Turning to the second question – does sinful man have any input into his own 'regeneration'? I think we need to consider carefully the Lord's words to Nicodemus in John chapter 3 where He declares the necessity of being 'born again' [i.e. 'regenerated'] for entry into the Kingdom of Heaven. In considering question one we read that in 'the communication of a *new life*' there were 'two operating powers' namely 'The Word of Truth' ['seed' – see Luke 8:11] and 'The Holy Spirit' [the 'quickening agent' – see John 6:63 and Romans 4:17]. When someone is born for the first time ['born of the flesh' – see John 3:6] there are likewise 'two operating powers' involved, namely the woman's 'seed' and the man's 'sperm'. If a child is conceived all the credit belongs to the Lord for we read in Psalm 127:3 'Lo, children are an heritage from the Lord; and the fruit of the womb is his reward'.

Any resultant offspring has had no input whatsoever into his 'first birth' and in like-fashion anyone graciously 'born again' ('born of the Spirit' – see John 3:6) has had no input into his own 'regeneration'. As we read in Jonah 2:9 and Psalm 3:8 'Salvation is of, and belongs to the Lord'. God does use other independent human agents to sow and water the 'seed' but as Paul explained in 1 Corinthians 3:6-7, any resultant 'fruit' is entirely due to God *alone* – 'I have planted, Apollos watered, but God gave the increase. So then, neither is he that planteth anything, neither he that watereth, but God giveth the increase'.

I often hear unregenerate people being urged to 'exercise faith' – but what is 'faith'? Well, we find the answer in Hebrews 11:1 'Now faith is the substance of things hoped for, the evidence of things not seen'. This is something a 'natural [unregenerate] man' (1 Corinthians 2:14) does not possess (and therefore cannot 'exercise') because such understanding and assurance comes only through the work of 'The Holy Spirit' (1 Corinthians 2:14) who must *first* 'quicken' (regenerate) the sinner who is 'dead in trespasses and sins' (Ephesians 2:1). Lazarus could not 'exercise faith' to initiate his 'coming forth' from the tomb (see John 11:17-44) – he first had to be 'quickened' (regenerated) by the voice of God ['Lazarus' – see John 11:43] and when the Lord called him by name he was 'reborn' and so could 'come forth' but He *first* had to be brought to life by God and it is exactly the same in the matter of 'spiritual regeneration'.

At this point let me say that if anyone promotes teaching on regeneration that is in conflict with what has been Biblically shown to be the truth on this matter of regeneration, if they accommodate in their thinking the necessity for some input by sinful man, whether in the form of a conscious decision coupled with religious ritual, then I believe they are promoting a 'false gospel' such as that anathematised by Paul in Galatians chapter 1. There, Paul, under inspiration, rejected the false teaching of a human decision to submit to 'ritualistic' circumcision as being necessary for salvation – 'And certain men which came down from Judea taught the brethren and said, Except ye be circumcised after the manner of Moses, ye cannot be saved' (Acts 15:1).

This was mirrored in one of the greatest modern-day errors committed by so-called 'evangelicals' in 1994 when they signed their agreement to the *Evangelicals and Catholics Together Agreement* – an agreement that in effect sanctioned two ways in which people could become Christians. One was the Biblical and true way as outlined in Vines' *Expository Dictionary* but the second was the false 'ritualistic' way as captured by these words from the agreement:

> 'Those converted, whether understood... as having experienced the reawakening of the new birth *originally bestowed in the sacrament of baptism...*'

This was a statement that Charles Colson, Bill Bright, J I Packer and other 'evangelicals' had no difficulty in publicly endorsing – what a betrayal of divine truth!

Now, how does C S Lewis view regeneration, namely 'the communication of a *new life*' as we learnt from Vine's definition? Let me turn again to his book *Mere Christianity* and there we read on page 59:

> 'In Christ a new kind of man appeared: and the new kind of life, which began in Him, is to be put into us.'

I have great difficulty with this statement for this reason: Jesus Christ was the *incarnate* Son of God whereas believers today are *regenerate* sons of God. To my way of thinking Mr Lewis is as wrong here as was Kenneth Hagin Snr when he taught 'Every man who has been born again is an incarnation and Christianity is a miracle. *The believer is as much an incarnation as was Jesus of Nazareth*' [Quoted by Hank Hanegraaff on page 383 of the hardback edition of his book *Christianity in Crisis*]. Jesus Christ was the *sinless incarnate* Son of God whereas believers are *sinful regenerate* sons of God – yes, believers now have 'spiritual life' and their personal hope and God's earnest desire is that they should 'be conformed to the image of his Son' (Romans 8:29) but we must never forget that the *incarnate* Son of God was *impeccable* whereas sadly, as we all know from bitter experience, believers are *regenerate* but *peccable* sons of God – 'If we say we have no sin, we deceive ourselves, and the truth is not in us' (1 John 1:8). Later on page 59 of *Mere Christianity* Mr Lewis writes:

> 'There are three things that spread the Christ life to us: baptism, belief, and that mysterious action *which different Christians* call by different names – Holy Communion, *the Mass*, the Lord's supper.'

When professing Christians use Christian terminology, their understanding of that terminology must be framed in the context of the 'faith community' with which they personally identify. (By way of example, when a Mormon speaks of 'salvation' he usually has 'resurrection' in view whereas a Christian would have an altogether different theological concept in mind). So when C S Lewis speaks of 'belief' sandwiched between 'baptism' and 'Holy Communion', it is patently evident that his 'belief' is that the reception of what he calls 'the Christ life' or what Christians would call *regeneration* comes to a person via a *sacramental system*. On page 62 of *Mere Christianity* he writes:

> 'This new life is spread not only by purely mental acts like belief, but by bodily acts like baptism and Holy Communion... God never meant man to be a purely spiritual creature. That is why He uses material things like bread and wine to put new life into us.'

These teachings would all be perfectly consistent with his own personal identity with the Anglican Church and also with his 'fellowship' with active, practising Roman Catholics. Each of their *sacramental systems* involve 'belief' or what I referred to earlier as 'a conscious decision coupled with religious ritual' and the reality is that such 'belief' has no concord with the biblical teaching on regeneration.

27

In the light of these teachings by C S Lewis I would once more challenge Derick Bingham's public assertion that Mr Lewis was 'our greatest Christian writer' for in the light of what we have considered to date I believe Mr Lewis was wrong in his teaching on repentance and regeneration, and we will now consider his teaching on redemption.

The teachings of C S Lewis on Redemption

One of the most glorious truths at the heart of the 'Gospel of Christ' is the message of redemption. It has gripped the hearts of hymn writers when they penned words like 'Redeemed how I love to proclaim it, redeemed by the blood of the lamb' and 'There is a redeemer, Jesus, God's own Son, precious lamb of God, Messiah, Holy One'.

I want to consider this matter of redemption from two angles – I want firstly to look at what C S Lewis believed about what I would call 'individual redemption' and then to look at what C S Lewis believed about what I would call 'corporate redemption'.

Before homing in on these two 'angles' let us first establish the clear Biblical meaning of 'redemption'. In his *Dictionary of Theological Terms*, Alan Cairns wrote:

> 'The deliverance of God's elect from a state of sin into a state of salvation by the means and merit of the ransom paid by Christ on their behalf.'

Mr Cairns went on to quote from John Owen's classic *Death of Death* (p 147):

> 'Redemption... is the delivery of any one from captivity and misery by the intervention "lutrou" of a price or ransom. That this ransom, or price of our deliverance was the blood of Christ is evident.'

Through the sacrificial shedding of His blood on the Cross of Calvary Christ paid a ransom price to purchase a '*group of people*' and so release them from their 'state of sin' [condemned] and bring them into a 'state of salvation' [justified]. We learn who this 'group of people' are when we read the words of Paul to the Ephesian Elders in Acts 20:28 'Take heed therefore unto yourselves, and to all the flock over the which the Holy Ghost hath made you overseers, to *feed the church, which he* [Christ] *hath purchased with his own blood'*.

'The Church' speaks of both 'individual' and 'corporate' redemption.

Not only do this *'group of people'*, the 'individuals' who 'corporately' make up 'The Church', now belong to Christ, but they also enjoy a special benefit that flows from that 'blood bought' Calvary transaction. John Murray, in his book, *Redemption: Accomplished and Applied* wrote:

> 'When Paul says that in the beloved "we have redemption through his blood, the forgiveness of sins" [Ephesians 1:7; Colossians 1:14], it is quite plain that he conceives the forgiveness of sins as the blessing accrued from blood redemption... the death of Christ is redemptively efficacious in reference to sin.'

The question we must consider is this. To what effective *extent* has Christ redeemed the 'individuals' who 'corporately' comprise 'The Church'? Is 'individual' redemption *plenary* or *partial*? Is 'corporate' redemption effectively limited only to 'The Church'?

Where 'individual' redemption is considered, the teaching of Scripture is clear. As far as an individual's 'sin' is concerned there is *plenary* [full] forgiveness and not *partial*. Twice in the book of Hebrews God spells out what has been accomplished in the realm of 'forgiveness' as a result of the redemptive work of Christ, *Who alone* is 'the mediator of the new covenant' (Hebrews 12:24). In Hebrews 8:12 God says 'their sins and their iniquities will I remember no more' and He repeats His promise in Hebrews 10:17.

When God forgives a true 'born again' believer, He forgives *fully* and that person is no longer under 'condemnation', which is the position of every unregenerate unbeliever – John 5:24 'verily, verily I say unto you, he that heareth my word and believeth on him that sent me hath everlasting life and shall not come into condemnation but is passed from death [condemned] unto life [justified]'.

In an article in the December 2003 *Evangelical Times* entitled *Why Was Jesus Born?* Peter Jeffrey cited the equivalent of a modern-day parable when he wrote:

> 'Christmas is probably the most expensive time of the year. All those presents... have to be paid for. When January comes and the credit card bills roll in, the full cost is seen. We may end up heavily in debt. But wait a moment, "Why Jesus Was Born" is about the cost God was willing to pay to remove your debt of sin. What if in January your credit card debt was *fully* paid by someone else... Your sin has run up an enormous "debt"... if you turn to Jesus and trust in His death for the forgiveness of your sin... you will find that Jesus has paid the debt [fully] for you. That is why He was born and that is why He died.'

Did C S Lewis teach that, for a believer, their 'debt was *fully* paid by someone else' – that 'someone else' being Jesus Christ and that upon death they would go immediately 'to be with Christ which is far better' (Philippians 1:23)? The answer sadly is a resounding '*No!*' On pages 109-111 of his book *Prayer: Letters to Malcolm*, C S Lewis wrote:

> 'Of course I pray for the dead. The action is so spontaneous, so all but inevitable, that only the most compulsive theological case against it would deter men [would "There is therefore no condemnation to those who are in Christ Jesus" (Romans 8:1) be a sufficiently "compulsive theological case against" praying for the dead?] And I hardly know how the rest of my prayers would survive if those for the dead were forbidden. At our age the majority of those we

love best are dead. What sort of intercourse with God could I have if what I love best were unmentionable to Him? On the traditional Protestant view, all the dead are damned or saved. If they are damned, prayer for them is useless. If they are saved, it is equally useless... To pray for them presupposes that progress and difficulty are still possible. In fact you are bringing in something like Purgatory. Well, I suppose I am... I believe in Purgatory... the very etymology [origin] of the word Purgatory has dropped out of sight. Its pains do not bring us nearer to God, but make us forget Him. It is a place not of purification but purely of retributive punishment [a wrong view in the opinion of C S Lewis]. The right view returns magnificently in Newman's *Dream*. There if I remember rightly, the saved soul, at the very foot of the throne, begs to be taken away and cleansed. It cannot bear for a moment longer "with its darkness to affront that light". Religion has reclaimed Purgatory. Our souls demand Purgatory, don't they? Would it not break the heart if God said to us "It is true, my son, that your breath smells and your rags drip with mud and slime, but we are charitable here and no one will upbraid you with these things, nor draw away from you. Enter into the joy"? [These sentiments are Biblically true because believers are "accepted in the beloved" (Ephesians 1:6) and "the blood of Jesus Christ his Son cleanseth us from all sin" (1 John 1:7).] Should we not reply "With submission sir, and if there is no objection, I'd rather be cleaned first". It may hurt you know – "Even so, sir". [Did C S Lewis never read what Paul wrote to vile sinners who had become believers? – "And such were some of you, but ye are *washed*, but ye are sanctified, but ye are justified in the name of the Lord Jesus and by the Spirit of our God" (1 Corinthians 6:11).] I assume that the process of purification will normally involve suffering... But I don't think suffering is the purpose of the purgation. I can well believe that people neither much worse nor much better than I will suffer less than I or more. No nonsense about merit. The treatment given will be the one required, whether it hurts little or much. My favourite image of this comes from the dentist's chair. I hope that when the tooth of life is drawn [death] and when I am coming round [entering eternity] a voice will say, "Rinse your mouth out with this". This will be Purgatory. The rinsing may take longer than I can now imagine. The taste of this may be more fiery and astringent than my present sensibility could endure. But More and Fisher shall not persuade me that it will be disgusting and unhallowed.'

These teachings of C S Lewis are a clear denial of the Biblical teachings of the inspired, revealed *extent* to which Christ has redeemed 'individuals'! But what about the effective *extent* of Christ's 'corporate' redemption – is it effectively limited only to that *'group of people'*, those 'individuals', who 'corporately' comprise 'The Church'?

The Bible teaches that only Christians, only those 'born again' (John 3:5), only those who 'by one Spirit... were all baptised into one body' (1 Corinthians 12:13) are members of 'The Church'. Commenting on this verse from Corinthians in an article in the January 2004 *Evangelical Times* entitled *Baptised by the Spirit*, Stan Evers wrote:

'Paul writes "by one baptism we were all baptised", but which baptism does he mean? Paul's words echo John the Baptist's prediction: "I indeed baptise you with water; but One mightier than I is coming, whose sandal strap I am not worthy to loose. He will baptise you with the Holy Spirit and fire" (Luke 3:16). We learn from John's words that there is a distinction

> between water baptism and Spirit baptism. The
> Spirit baptism places us into *Christ's body, the*
> *church* [Paul writes "And he [Christ] is the head
> of *the body, the church*" (Colossians 1:18)].
> Water baptism is a public declaration that we are
> in Christ's body.'

The Apostle Paul knew and taught that only those who had 'Jesus
Christ and Him crucified' (1 Corinthians 2:2) preached to them
and who were 'quickened' [brought to spiritual life] (Ephesians
2:1) and who were 'baptised' (1 Corinthians 12:13) by that 'one
spirit' were in 'the body, the church' and belonged to Christ, for
he wrote in Romans 8:9 'If any man have not the Spirit of Christ,
he is none of his'. This is why Paul wrote so passionately of
missionary endeavour in Romans 10:13-15 'For whosoever shall
call upon the name of the Lord shall be saved. How then shall
they call on him in whom they have not believed? And how shall
they believe in him of whom they have not heard? And how shall
they hear without a preacher. And how shall they preach except
they be sent.' Paul knew that 'the gospel of Christ… is the power
of God unto salvation' (Romans 1:16) and that 'it pleased God by
the foolishness of preaching to save them that believe'. If there is
no preaching of 'the gospel of Christ' there will be no belief 'in
Him' and no one can be 'saved'.

So, the effective *extent* of Christ's 'corporate' redemption,
according to the Bible, is limited to those who have 'the gospel
of Christ' preached to them and who by the work of the Holy
Spirit are subsequently 'converted' (Matthew 18:3). Did C S
Lewis believe and teach that? Again, sadly, the answer is yet
another resounding '*No!*'.

On page 173 of *Mere Christianity* C S Lewis wrote:

> 'There are people in other religions who are being
> led by God's secret influence to concentrate on
> those parts of their religion which are in
> agreement with Christianity and *who thus belong*
> *to Christ without knowing it.* For example, a
> Buddhist of good will may be led to concentrate
> more and more on the Buddhist teaching about

mercy and to leave in the background (although he might still say he believed) the Buddhist teaching on certain other points. Many of the good Pagans long before Christ's birth may have been in this position... Consequently it is not much use trying to make judgments about Christians and non-Christians in the mass.' [If this were true then there would be no point in sending missionaries to 'merciful Buddhists' and 'good Pagans'.]

These teachings of C S Lewis are a clear denial of the Biblical teachings of the inspired, revealed effective *extent* of Christ's 'corporate' redemption of 'The Church'. I think the simplest overall way to summarise the false teachings of C S Lewis on these points is to say that he has *under-estimated individual redemption* and *over-estimated corporate redemption*.

Conclusion

When we examine Biblically the teachings of C S Lewis on redemption and also consider his teachings on repentance and regeneration that we previously looked at, we must really wonder how it came to be that someone as highly esteemed in 'evangelical' circles as Derick Bingham actually described C S Lewis as 'our greatest Christian writer'.

In an article in the January 2002 *Evangelical Times*, Roger Fay, a Pastor in Ripon, England, who is not given to the use of excessively inflammatory language, wrote:

'It is debatable whether C S Lewis was regenerate.'

In an article entitled *Did C S Lewis Go To Heaven*? John Robbins of The Trinity Foundation, wrote:

'Did C S Lewis go to Heaven? Our answer must be: Not if he believed what he wrote in his books and letters.'

In the light of my own studies I would certainly not agree with Derick Bingham's assessment of C S Lewis and I would require a lot of Biblical convincing to disagree with the sentiments of either Roger Fay or John Robbins.

2

Philip Yancey—'turning the grace of God into lasciviousness'?

Introduction

When you go into any modern 'Christian' bookstore it will be virtually impossible not to be confronted at some point by books written by Philip Yancey. He is without doubt one of the best selling 'Christian' authors of this age. Some of his best known works include *What's So amazing About Grace?*, *Where Is God When It Hurts?* and *Soul Survivor*. In March 2002 he was the Banquet Speaker at the Christian Booksellers Convention held in Doncaster.

As a freelance 'Christian' writer he serves as Editor at Large for the pseudo-evangelical publication *Christianity Today*. His writings have (rightly) attracted criticism and controversy from 'conservative' Christians despite a claim by Yancey in an article published on 21 September 2002 by Alf McCreary (Religious Affairs Correspondent of the *Belfast Telegraph*) that 'My calling is not to be successful but to be faithful to God'.

Yancey's views on homosexuality

One of the areas where his 'faithfulness to God' has been challenged has been in how he views homosexuality and lesbianism and its compatibility with the professed Christianity of those who pursue such life-styles. In relation to his book *What's So Amazing About Grace?* I have on file some comments made about it by two Christians.

One report was sent to me by an 'ordinary' Christian lady called Mona and in it Mona wrote:

> 'This writer [Yancey] gives a long, involved portion of his book reasoning in favour of

homosexuality based on his strong friendship with this "Christian" [Mel White] who left his wife to resume a homosexual lifestyle which he could not resist. At the same time Christian "hate" attitudes are reviled, and while these may not be endorsed, neither is there justification for what God calls an abomination, nor is there any Biblical injunction to "pour grace on it" [homosexuality].'

Mona told of how Yancey accompanied his 'gay Christian' friend Mel White on the 'gay' march in Washington in March 1987 and how Yancey 'relates the shocking behaviour of Christian protesters at the march, but commends the "gay Christian" response – "Jesus Loves Us"'.

In the other report written by Pastor Gary Gilley of Southern View Chapel, Pastor Gilley wrote:

'Yancey has a fundamental flaw that runs throughout all of his writings – he doesn't always draw his thoughts and principles from Scripture... this serious flaw of not basing his concepts squarely upon the Scriptures eventually leads Yancey astray. Yancey does not know the difference between tolerance and arrogance; between grace and license; between boldness and harshness. By Yancey's definitions John the Baptist and Elijah would be men of "ungrace" but God did not seem to think so... Certainly Jesus loved and spent time with prostitutes, but He did so to call them to repentance, not to accept their way of living. Yancey's method of dealing with a homosexual, who is also a church leader, may seem like "grace" to him, it may seem like what Jesus would do, but it is clearly out of sync with the teachings and examples of Scripture.'

In recent days I was sent the transcript of an interview with Philip Yancey that is posted on the website of a 'ministry' called *Whosoever* <http://www.whosoever.org/index.shtml>.

Whosoever is subtitled *An online magazine for Gay, Lesbian, Bisexual and Transgender Christians.*

From the *What We Believe* section of the website much can be learned of how this 'ministry' views the teaching, authority and relevance of the Word of God and as you read some extracts of their statement (with my own comments added) perhaps, like me, you will be reminded of how Peter warned of people who being 'unlearned and unstable, wrest [twist] as they do also the other scriptures, unto their own destruction' (2 Peter 3:16).

Point 3 states:

> 'We are called by God to never return evil for evil, and to turn the other cheek. We can expect persecution as gay, lesbian, bisexual or transgendered Christians. But we are warned not to stoop to the level of our persecutors.
>
> Luke 6:27-29 – "Love your enemies, do good to those who hate you, bless those who curse you, pray for those who abuse you. To those who strike you on the cheek, offer the other also."
>
> Romans 12:14 – "Bless those who persecute you; bless and do not curse them."
>
> John 15:18-19 – "If the world hates you, know that it has hated me before it hated you. If you were of the world, the world would love its own; but because you are not of the world, but I chose you of the world, therefore the world hates you."'

Comments: The Scriptures quoted here are the Lord's instructions to true disciples as to how they should behave when they suffer for living a Holy, Faithful, Godly, and Christian life. Paul states that 'all that will live godly in Christ Jesus shall suffer persecution' (2 Timothy 3:12). Whilst not in any way condoning 'persecution' of gays etc. (whether by professing Christians or by the world at large) the point to note is that they are not being persecuted for 'living godly in Christ Jesus' and they cannot therefore appropriate these scriptures to themselves as a defence.

Point 4 of the statement declares:

> 'We believe that salvation is between God and the individual and is not open to criticism, question or judgment by others. We believe faith in Jesus Christ is the only justification needed.
>
> Philippians 2:12 – "Wherefore, my beloved, as ye have always obeyed, not as in my presence only, but now much more in my absence, work out your own salvation with fear and trembling."
>
> Ephesians 2:8-9 – "For by grace are ye saved through faith; and that not of yourselves: it is the gift of God: Not of works, lest any man should boast."
>
> Galatians 2:21 – "I do not frustrate the grace of God: for if righteousness come by the law, then Christ is dead in vain."'

Comments: It is true that 'salvation' is not based on 'human works' but the 'human works' of those professing to be Christians will evidence true 'salvation'. God's word encourages Christians to 'test the spirits whether they are of God' (1 John 4:1). The validity of someone's profession of being a Christian can be tested by 'their fruits' (Matthew 7:20) so God's Word not only sanctions 'criticism, question and judgment' but commends it: 'Brethren, if any one of you do err from the truth and one convert him, Let him know that he who converteth the sinner from the error of his way shall save a soul from death and shall hide a multitude of sins' (James 5:19-20). Paul didn't hold back from telling professing Christians in Ephesus how they should live in the light of their claimed conversion as we read in Ephesians 4:17-24. In verses 17 and 19 he says 'walk not as other gentiles walk... who being past feeling [having no conscience] have given themselves over unto lasciviousness' and in verse 24 he says 'put on the new man, which after God is created in righteousness and true holiness' –

Paul expected to see the 'fruits' of genuine conversion to Christ in the lives of these professing Christians.

Point 5 states:

> 'We believe that we are all equal in the eyes of God, regardless of sexual orientation.
>
> Galatians 3:28 – "There is neither Jew nor Greek, there is neither bond nor free, there is neither male nor female: for ye are all one in Christ Jesus."'

Comments: Galatians 3:28 teaches the 'equal standing' before God of all true believers, irrespective of their racial background, their social background or their God-given gender. It does not teach an 'equal standing' before God for all, irrespective of their moral life style. The Apostle Paul, writing to the Corinthian Church that was plagued by problems of immorality, said 'Be not deceived: neither fornicators, nor idolaters, nor adulterers, nor effeminate, nor abusers of themselves with mankind... shall inherit the kingdom of God' (1 Corinthians 6:9-10).

Point 6 states:

> 'We believe God made us as gays, lesbians, bisexuals, and transgendered persons and has opened God's realm to us without reservation.
>
> John 15:16-17 – "You did not choose me, but I chose you and appointed you that you should go and bear fruit and that your fruit should abide; so that whatever you ask the Father (Heavenly Parent) in my name, God may give it to you. This I command you, to love one another."'

Comments: This statement fails to take into account that the pinnacle of God's 'good' creation (Genesis 1:31) was humanity – 'male and female' (Genesis 1:27) and that the only sexual relationship blessed by God was that between man and woman (Genesis 2:24). In Hebrews 13:4 we read 'Marriage is honourable among all, and the bed [the place of sexual intimacy] undefiled'. Pastor John MacArthur comments 'God highly honours marriage which He instituted at creation... Sexual activity in a marriage is pure but any sexual activity outside marriage brings one under divine judgment. God prescribes serious consequences for sexual immorality'. Any deviation in moral behaviour from God's 'good' pattern came as a result of the entrance of sin as detailed in Genesis 3 and God does not bless such sin, as many passages in the Word of God teach clearly. A passage such as Romans 1:18-32 teaches that God did not 'open God's realm' to immoral sinners but rather God 'gave them up [abandoned them]' (verses 24, 26 and 28) to their sinful lusts.

Point 7 states:

> 'We believe the Bible is the inspired word of God that must be read in the context it was written. Many of its truths are universal and can be directly applied to modern times. But a majority of canonical scripture is situation and time specific to the culture of its time. Therefore, one must use exegesis and prayerful communion with the Holy Spirit before applying canonical scripture to today's culture.
>
> 1 Corinthians 2:10-13 – "God has revealed to us through the Spirit. For the Spirit searches everything, even the depths of God. For what person knows another person's thoughts except the spirit of the person which is in them? So also no one comprehends the thoughts of God except the spirit of God. Now we have received not the spirit of the world, but the Spirit of God, that we might understand the gifts bestowed on us by God. And we impart this in words not taught by human wisdom but taught by the Spirit, interpreting spiritual truths to those who possess the Spirit."'

Comments: The ongoing authority and application of God's Word is taught in the Scriptures themselves. The Apostle Paul wrote in his last letter before being martyred for the Gospel 'All scripture is given by inspiration of God, and is profitable for doctrine, for reproof, for correction, for instruction in righteousness: That the man of God may be perfect, throughly furnished unto all good works' (2 Timothy 3:16-17). Speaking of His second coming, the Lord Himself said 'Heaven and earth shall pass away but my words shall not pass away' (Luke 21:33) and four chapters earlier, when again speaking of His second coming, He likened future conditions to those of 'the days of Lot' when God, angered by the immorality of Sodom, 'rained fire and brimstone from heaven and destroyed them all' (Luke 17:28-29). God's view of sinful immorality is not 'situation and time specific' but eternal 'truth' (John 17:17) because 'Forever, O Lord, thy word is settled in heaven' (Psalm 119:89). Unrepentant 'fornicators' of whatever 'orientation' will spend eternity in 'the lake which burneth with fire' and will find the door of 'the Holy city, new Jerusalem' permanently closed to them 'for outside are... fornicators' (Revelation 21:8; 21:2; 22:15).

Point 8 states:

> 'We believe God is alive and is speaking to God's children even today. God's words are found in the Bible but God continues to reveal truths not found in scripture through the Holy Spirit.
>
> Hebrews 4:12 - "For the word of God is living and active, sharper than a two edged sword, piercing to the division of soul and spirit, of joints and marrow, and discerning the thoughts and intentions of the heart."'

Comments: The Word of God teaches that Christians are not to seek 'truths not found in scripture'. The Apostle Paul instructed believers 'not to think above that which is written' (1 Corinthians 4:6) and there is another clear warning to God's people that teaches 'Add thou not unto his words, lest he reprove thee and thou be found a liar' (Proverbs 30:6). The same book of Hebrews quoted in this point 8 of the statement also teaches how God spoke in Old Testament times but how He has now finally spoken to the world through His Son –

'God, who at sundry times and in divers manners spake in time past unto the fathers by the prophets, Hath in these last days spoken unto us by his Son' (Hebrews 1:1-2). Bible commentator, F B Hole wrote 'We are at once brought face to face with the tremendous fact that God, who had spoken to the fathers of Israel by prophets in former days, had now spoken in divine fullness and with finality in His Son' (Epistles: Vol: 3: pages 1-2).

Moving on from the *What We Believe* section of the website I want to comment upon the interviewer who is referred to on the website as the 'Rev.' Candace Chellew-Hodge. Her personal details, beside her photo (in clerical robes) include:

> 'Candace is the last of five kids of a Southern Baptist minister, and is herself ordained through Gentle Spirit Christian Church of Atlanta, Georgia. She has worked in journalism and public relations for nearly 20 years. She founded Whosoever because "there were simply no good Christian magazines to read that didn't bash gays at some point." She and her partner, Wanda, live in the sticks of South Carolina with way too many cats and dogs.'

At the conclusion of the interview posted to the website we read the following:

> 'Candace Chellew-Hodge is a recovering Southern Baptist and founder/editor of Whosoever: An Online Magazine for GLBT Christians. She is an ordained minister and holds a master's in theological studies from the Candler School of Theology at Emory University in Atlanta, Ga. She is a spiritual director trained through the Episcopal Diocese of Atlanta. She has worked for the past two decades in journalism and public relations.'

The fact that this lady styles herself as 'Rev.' shows her disobedience to the prohibitions of the Bible concerning women and teaching (see 1 Timothy 2:12). As you will have read in the title to this part, I have quoted Jude 4 that speaks of 'certain men [who] crept in unawares [secretly, who escaped notice]... ungodly men, turning the grace of God into lasciviousness'.

The problem of 'lasciviousness' amongst professing believers is something that the Scriptures pay much attention to. We must first understand what 'lasciviousness' is and Vine's *Expository Dictionary* defines the word on page 353 as denoting 'excess, licentiousness, absence of restraint, indecency, wantonness... one of the evils that proceed from the heart [Mark 7:22]; one of the evils of which some in the church at Corinth had been guilty of [2 Corinthians 12:21]; classed among the works of the flesh [Galatians 5:19]; among the sins of the unregenerate who are "past feeling" [Ephesians 4:19]; one of the sins against which believers are warned [Romans 13:13]'. Vine also links the 'pernicious ways' of 2 Peter 2:2 to 'lasciviousness' and to the 'filthy manner of life of the wicked' in Sodom and Gomorrah from which Lot was 'delivered' [2 Peter 2:6-7]. Vine concludes 'The prominent idea is shameless conduct'.

In the light of this website's *What We Believe* section, I believe it is clear that those involved in and sympathetic to this 'ministry' are seeking to justify a life style that the Bible condemns as 'lasciviousness'. What I want to address now is the interview given by Philip Yancey to the 'Rev.' Candace Chellew-Hodge and to consider whether Mr Yancey is likewise guilty of 'turning the grace of God into lasciviousness'. The preamble to the interview, written by 'Rev.' Candace Chellew-Hodge is itself quite enlightening as it reveals how she changed her initial perception of Mr Yancey as a result of reading some of his books. In the preamble Candace Chellew-Hodge wrote:

> 'I first heard of Philip Yancey when his book
> "What's So Amazing About Grace?" came out in
> 1997. Even though many people whom I
> respected raved about the book, I was not
> interested in reading the book. Why would I? It
> was written by a man who regularly wrote for
> Christianity Today – a magazine that was less

than gay friendly. I'm not one to spend my precious reading time on authors who bash gays and lesbians – or authors that I perceive might do that. I know their positions and their arguments. Reading their books seemed like a waste of time. I must now confess that I unfairly judged Yancey. I let a silly "guilt-by-association" taint my opinion of him even before giving his books a chance. I regret that, but perhaps God knows best. If I had read Yancey in 1997 I might not have appreciated his gentleness, his grace or his mercy quite as much as I do now. I finally gave in and read Yancey's work only after I had subscribed to the audio book service Audible... Audible has a great selection of Christian and spiritual books and I've consumed most of their catalogue. It was during a dry spell, when I had exhausted much of the collection that interested me that I turned to Yancey's new book, "Rumours of Another World". I had been in spiritual crisis and was looking for someone to explain to me how to reach that supernatural world that we know exists, but somehow cannot relate to or forget about in our daily rush. The description of the book sounded intriguing so I put my preconceived notions of Yancey aside and downloaded the book. What a blessing! The book was just what I needed. I did, however, cringe through the chapter on "Designer Sex" waiting for that bash against gays and lesbians. It never came. I was deeply shocked – an evangelical who didn't use a chapter on sex to take a pot shot at homosexuals? It was hard to imagine. The tone of the book led me to make another selection by Yancey. "Reaching for the Invisible God" was another book I listened to with an eager hunger. Finally, an author offered an intelligent treatment of faith, doubt and how we relate to a God we cannot see. I was beginning to see why so many people loved

Yancey – and why others would not like him at all – especially if they clung to a fundamentalist, black and white faith. Finally, I decided to read "Grace". This book left me speechless and utterly blessed. I want to start a church based solely on the teachings of this book – of God's "grace on tap" for every person who walks through the door. I think it should be required reading for every single church member on the face of the earth... It was Yancey's description of his friendship with Mel White in "Grace" that touched me most deeply. White's story, documented in his own book "Stranger at the Gate", has been well documented in the gay and lesbian community... Shunned by his former employees, White went on to found "Soulforce", a social action group dedicated to the spiritual equality of gay, lesbian, bisexual and transgender believers. Yancey's steadfast support for his friend Mel, and *his own struggle with the sinfulness of homosexuality* is documented in the book and is one of the most honest accounts of grace in the face of struggle that I believe I have ever read. It was this chapter that led me to write to Yancey and tell him how much his books had moved me. He was kind enough to send me a reply that emboldened me to ask for an interview. He agreed to an email interview, given his busy schedule. I was amazed that he would lend his name to a publication like "Whosoever" – and eternally grateful. I cannot recommend his work strongly enough. If you thirst for grace, peace and joy, read Yancey's works. You will not be disappointed.'

*I can confirm (as the result of email exchanges with Candace Chellew-Hodge) that the phrase in this preamble 'his own struggle with the sinfulness of homosexuality' does refer to

Philip Yancey's 'struggle' and not to any 'struggle' by his homosexual friend, Mel White.

It is not my intention to publish and analyze in full the interview given, but rather to quote extracts and to make comments. The full interview, detailing all the questions posed by Candace Chellew-Hodge of *Whosoever* and setting out, in full, the answers given by Philip Yancey can be viewed by following this link: <http://www.whosoever.org/v8i6/yancey.shtml>.

Question by Whosoever:

> 'In your book "What's so Amazing about Grace?" you tell about your friendship with "Soulforce" leader Mel White and your support of him at the ["gay"] March on Washington in 1987... What is your position on gays and lesbians in the church?'

Answer by Yancey:

> '...Mel was one of my closest friends for years before he revealed to me his sexual orientation. (He still is, by the way.) He had repressed and hidden his homosexuality, and in fact was married and was making a fine career in Christian publishing and ministry... I get hate letters full of equal venom from both sides: from conservative Christians appalled that I would maintain a friendship with Mel and write compassionately about gays and lesbians, and from the other side wishing I would go further with a full endorsement... I'm sure of what my own attitude should be toward gays and lesbians: I should show love and grace. As one person told me, "Christians get very angry toward other Christians who sin differently than they do." When people ask me how I can possibly stay friends with a sinner like Mel, I respond by asking how Mel can possibly stay friends with a sinner like me. Even if I conclude that all homosexual behaviour is wrong, as many conservative Christians do, I'm still

compelled to respond with love. As I've attended
gay and lesbian churches, I'm also saddened that
the evangelical church by and large finds no place
for homosexuals. I've met wonderful, committed
Christians who attend **MCC churches, and I
wish that the larger church had the benefit of their
faith. And at the same time, I think it's unhealthy to
have an entire denomination formed around this
one particular issue--those people need exposure to
and inclusion in the wider Body of Christ. When it
gets to particular matters of policy, like ordaining
gay and lesbian ministers, I'm confused, like a lot
of people. There are a few--not many, but a few
passages of Scripture that give me pause. Frankly,
I don't know the answer to those questions. My
church in Chicago spent a couple of years carefully
studying the issue. The church had openly gay
members, but did not allow practicing
homosexuals in leadership positions (as they did
not allow unmarried "practicing heterosexuals,"
whatever that means). The committee studying the
issue looked at the biblical and theological and
social aspects and finally came down in the same
place: welcoming but not affirming homosexuals
in leadership roles. Conservatives got mad and left.
Many gays and lesbians also left, hurt that the
church reinforced their "second-class citizen"
status. I don't have a magic answer, and I can't see
one on the near horizon. Whole denominations are
struggling with the very same issue, as you know.'

**MCC refers to what is known as the Metropolitan Community
Church and from the website of the MCC in West Hollywood,
California we read the following:

'The first Metropolitan Community Churches
(MCC) was founded by Rev Troy D. Perry in
1968 in Los Angeles, CA (USA). This Fellowship
of Churches plays a vital role in addressing the
spiritual needs of the lesbian, gay, bisexual, and

transgender community around the world. For those of us who were raised in a religious atmosphere, homosexuality was usually associated with shame and guilt. As a result, many of us were cut off from the spiritual dimension of our lives. Metropolitan Community Churches provide an opportunity to explore a spiritual experience that affirms who we are.'

Comments: From the answer given by Mr Yancey the following conclusions can be drawn:

1. Mr Yancey asserts that sexually active professing 'gay Christians' are to be shown 'love and grace' and not to be challenged about their sexual activity and are to be viewed simply as Christians who *may be sinning* in a different manner to other Christians. Mr Yancey is clearly uncertain about whether homosexuality etc. is sinful in the light of his phraseology such as 'Even if', 'I'm confused', 'there are a few passages of scripture that give me pause' and 'I don't have a magic answer'.

2. The concept of 'gay and lesbian *churches*' appears to pose no theological problem for Mr Yancey. He views the Metropolitan Community Church as a bona-fide Christian 'denomination'. He appears to have acquiesced to the willingness of the Church he belonged to in Chicago accepting 'openly gay *members*' even though they did prohibit such from leadership roles.

3. Despite being a hugely successful 'Christian' writer Mr Yancey appears not to understand the term 'unmarried practising heterosexuals'. Someone in his position and with his influence should surely know that the Bible identifies such people as 'fornicators' [Fornication: In its more restricted sense fornication denotes voluntary sexual communion between an unmarried person and one of the opposite sex – Marshall Pickering *Evangelical Dictionary of Theology* page 422].

4. Mr Yancey reduces the *many passages* of Scripture that identify sexual activity outside the confines of the God-ordained marriage relationship of one man and one woman (Genesis 1:27-28 and Genesis 2:24) as being sinful to 'there are a *few passages* of scripture that give me pause'. In the use of this terminology I hear echoes of 'Yea, hath God Said?' (Genesis 3:1).

Question by Whosoever:

'How can other Evangelical Christians develop an attitude of grace (if not acceptance) toward gay and lesbian Christians?'

Answer by Yancey:

'The only way is through personal exposure. It's amazing how feelings change when suddenly it's your daughter or your brother who comes out of the closet. In my case, it was my friend Mel. The issues I had read about suddenly had a face, a person with a story. When that happened, everything changed. That's one reason why I think it's sad that the churches have so little contact. I have attended gay and lesbian churches whose fervency and commitment would put most evangelical churches to shame. Disapproving conservatives should have contact with those people, and vice versa.'

Comments: From the answer given by Mr Yancey the following conclusions can be drawn:

1. The concept of unrepentant 'gay and lesbian Christians' is obviously acceptable to Mr Yancey who commends them for their 'fervency and commitment'.

2. The phrase 'attitude of grace' appears to be interpreted by Mr Yancey as the eradication of 'Evangelical' Christian disapproval of homosexual/lesbian sexual activity – activity that the Bible clearly identifies as sinful. In effect Mr Yancey is encouraging an attitude of (to paraphrase

Isaiah 5:20) 'accepting evil as good'. God's 'grace' never involves 'accepting evil as good' and Mr Yancey is encouraging an attitude and approach to sin that Paul warned against in Romans 6:1-2 'What shall we say then? Shall we continue in sin that grace may abound? God forbid. How shall we [true Christians] that are dead to sin, live any longer in it?' Matthew Henry in his commentary on these verses wrote 'The apostle is very full in pressing the necessity of holiness... he shows that connection between justification and holiness are inseparable. Let the thought be abhorred, of continuing in sin that grace may abound. True believers are dead to sin; therefore they ought not to follow it. No man can at the same time be both dead and alive. He is a fool who, desiring to be dead unto sin, thinks he may live in it.

3. Mr Yancey encourages 'disapproving conservatives' to 'have contact with these people' – he obviously means for 'conservative' Christians to tolerate such sinful practices amongst professing Christians by having what he calls 'contact' with such people rather than disapprovingly confronting them. This advice by Mr Yancey conflicts with the Biblical commendation expressed in James 5:19-20 – 'Brethren, if any of you do err from the truth, and one convert him; Let him know, that he which converteth the sinner from the error of his way shall save a soul from death, and shall hide a multitude of sins.' – and with the concern expressed by Paul, who didn't tolerate sinful sexual, immoral activity by professing Christians, but rather declared that he would 'bewail' [lament and mourn over] those engaged in such sin (2 Corinthians 12:21).

Question by Whosoever:

> 'When my [lesbian] partner and I moved to a new state, we began searching for a church home. I wrote a letter to the local Episcopal rector explaining who we were and asked if we would be welcome in his church. His response, in a nutshell, was that we would be very welcome, if

only we gave up our "sinful lifestyle" and sought out good, Christian (presumably Episcopalian) men to marry. This is the reaction of many Christian churches to gays and lesbians. We must give up our sexual orientation to be accepted. What do you say to churches like this?'

Answer by Yancey:

'I'm probably not the best person to address a church like that--you are. Obviously, if a church is saying you need to give up sexual orientation, that church needs some education. I know of some ministries who try to change sexual behaviour, but none that try to change sexual orientation... I would probably approach that rector differently. I would point to how Jesus dealt with people who were moral failures--I'm starting where the rector is, who sees you as a moral failure. Jesus chose one such woman, a woman who had had five failed marriages, as his first missionary. I would also ask if he requires all who attend his church to leave their "sins" at the door.'

Comments: From the answer given by Mr Yancey the following conclusions can be drawn:

1. Mr Yancey clearly accepts the notion of diverse sexual orientation because very subtly the questioner has directed attention to what she calls 'sexual orientation' and diverted attention away from 'sexual activity'. This 'orientation' approach seeks to legitimise 'sexual activity' between those of the same gender by suggesting that diverse 'sexual orientation' is a perfectly normal and an integral part of God's 'good' created order. God's 'good' created order included humans created 'male and female' (Genesis 1:27) and there was no mention whatsoever of what might be termed 'cross orientation'. The 'sexual activity' attributed to this 'cross orientation' (homosexuality and lesbianism) is regularly identified in many passages of the Bible as an 'abomination' in the sight of God.

2. Mr Yancey identifies a woman (see John 4:1-29) who had 'five failed marriages' as a 'moral failure' and explains how Jesus chose her to be 'his first missionary'. Does Mr Yancey want to convey the impression that Jesus would use as a 'missionary' someone who was still enmeshed and wedded to sinful immorality? Has Mr Yancey forgotten the Lord's words to another 'moral failure' when he said to the woman who had been caught in the very act of adultery 'go and sin no more' (John 8:11). In Paul's second letter to Timothy he instructs those who 'name the name of Christ [to] depart from iniquity' so that they may be 'a vessel unto honour, sanctified and fit for the master's use' (2 Timothy 2:19, 21).

Conclusion

Much more could be written, not only on this topic of homosexuality and lesbianism but also about other worrying aspects of Mr Yancey's thinking when he makes statements like 'I also find a lot of spiritual nourishment in Catholic writers across the centuries. They understand the mystery, and many of them spent their entire lives exploring that mystery' and when the interviewer makes comments like: 'Your books convey an obvious intelligence and depth about your faith. You incorporate the thoughts of many serious theologians including Soren Kirkegaard, Simone Weil and Thomas Merton'.

Leaving these additional concerns aside and returning to Mr Yancey's comments on this whole issue of 'gay and lesbian Christians' I firmly believe that there is only one conclusion that can be arrived at. Measuring Mr Yancey's comments against the teaching of the Word of God, Mr Yancey is guilty of what Jude warned against in verse 4, namely of 'turning the grace of God into lasciviousness'. Mr Yancey is either not equipped or simply unwilling to articulate God's clear views on this moral issue and as a result he is giving false spiritual hope and comfort to those who are in danger of suffering the same judgment as their 'sexually orientated ancestors' as we read in Jude 7 of 'Sodom and Gomorrah, and the cities about them in like manner, giving themselves over to fornication and going after strange flesh, are set forth, for an example, suffering the vengeance of eternal fire'.

3

Alpha—Attend or Avoid?

Introduction

In recent years the Alpha course has become virtually a byword for introducing people to the Christian faith. Alpha started life in 1977 as a modest, local church based initiative, described as 'a means of presenting the basic principles of the Christian faith in a relaxed and informal setting'. Its home was then, and still is today, the Anglican Parish of Holy Trinity Brompton in London. Its first presenter was a man called Charles Marnham but today 'the face' of Alpha is the assistant curate, Nicky Gumbel, and to a lesser extent his boss, the vicar of Holy Trinity Brompton, Sandy Millar.

As a first step in our assessment I want to quote a short passage from Paul's second letter to Timothy.

> 'Thou therefore, my son, be strong in the grace that is in Christ Jesus. And the things that thou hast heard of me among many witnesses, the same commit thou to faithful men, who shall be able to teach others also.' (2 Timothy 2:1-2)

Donald Guthrie, on page 151 of his commentary writes:

> 'The idea is clearly to entrust something to another for safekeeping... The transmission of Christian truth must never be left to chance... and is... committed... only to reliable men who will also be qualified to teach others.'

All around the world, in a multitude of churches, representing a multitude of denominations, Alpha courses are being run. In these courses, the teaching of the Christian faith is being set aside by the local church eldership, and, by the use of a series of fifteen videos, is being entrusted into the hands of the Holy Trinity Brompton promoters and presenters of Alpha.

The question we need to consider is this: are men such as Sandy Millar and Nicky Gumbel 'reliable men' or 'faithful men' as Paul wrote to Timothy?

The 'Toronto Blessing'

Earlier, I said that Alpha first appeared in 1977, but in the mid 1990s, thanks to the efforts and input of Nicky Gumbel, it had what would be described in modern terminology as a bit of a makeover. This makeover, and the re-launching of Alpha, just happened to coincide with another event that was taking the then professing Christian world by storm – the so-called Toronto Blessing.

How did men like Sandy Millar and Nicky Gumbel react to the devilish claims of the Toronto Blessing? *Time* magazine carried a report in its issue of 15 August 1994 called *Laughing for the Lord*, and part of it said:

> 'It's Sunday evening in London's fashionable Knightsbridge neighbourhood. Though pathetically tiny flocks of Londoners attend many Anglican services, Holy Trinity Brompton has a standing-room-only turnout of 1500... After the usual Scripture readings, prayers and singing, the chairs are cleared away. Curate Nicky Gumbel prays that the Holy Spirit will come upon the congregation. Soon a woman begins laughing. Others gradually join her with hearty belly laughs. A young worshipper falls to the floor, hands twitching. Another falls, then another and another. Within half an hour there are bodies everywhere as supplicants sob, shake, roar like lions, and strangest of all, laugh uncontrollably. This frenzied display has become known as the "laughing revival" or "Toronto Blessing"... After first appearing at Holy Trinity only last May, laughing revivals have been reported in Anglican

parishes from Manchester to York to Brighton...
At London's Holy Trinity, schoolteacher Denise
Williams says she "came here a little sceptical"
but soon was caught up in the fervour. "There
was a lovely feeling of warmth and peace"...
lines outside Holy Trinity now start forming an
hour and a half before services.'

In September 1994 on Ulster Television's *Sunday Matters* a
panel discussion was chaired by Sue Cooke and I made
reference to it in a little booklet that I wrote called *The Toronto
Blessing is No Laughing Matter*.

This is part of what I wrote then:

'Amongst those taking part in the debate were a
husband and wife team. The wife had been a
"charismatic" Christian for a number of years but
her husband declared that he had been an
atheist... at a recent meeting where "Toronto-
Linked" phenomena were breaking out he
decided, rather reluctantly to go forward for
prayer and this is how Robert described what
happened:

"God for me was a historical figure but having
seen what *it* did to my own wife and to other
people *I can see that God was a living force* and
touching people. I had to rethink my life and
when I finally had the courage to go forward for
prayer I found myself saying 'God come into my
life'... since then I've been forward for prayer
other times and I've, yes, I've fallen down but
what *it's* made me do *is get in touch with
myself*... I came to God with fear because I
didn't know what was going to happen and I
resisted the falling down, *but I felt a force that
moved*" [demonstrating a pushing movement as
he spoke]...

Later Sue Cooke addressed... Nicky and said to him: "Nicky... long-term this kind of thing has happened before in history and then it has disappeared" – In reply Nicky said:

"Well I think we have to look to the fruit... we're seeing people's lives changed – I mean Robert is an example of someone who came as an atheist and his life was changed *through an encounter with Jesus Christ."'*

In response to this claim by Nicky Gumbel that Robert had had an encounter with Jesus Christ I wrote:

'Examine carefully what Robert said and you will find *no mention of Jesus Christ* – all you find are "New Age ideas" of God as *"it"*, *"a living force"*, making me *"get in touch with myself"*. There was no evidence of the true *Holy Spirit* glorifying Christ or "taking of the things of Christ and revealing them" (John 16:14).'

For Nicky Gumbel to interpret what Robert said as *an encounter with Jesus Christ* shows his total lack of discernment and his capacity to move comfortably in the world of what we now call 'the spin doctors' – in this case it was on behalf of the so-called 'Toronto Blessing'.

In an article in the Charismatic magazine *Renewal* in May 1995, Nicky Gumbel wrote:

'I believe it is no coincidence that the present movement of the Holy Spirit [referring to the Toronto Blessing] has come at the same time as the explosion of the Alpha Courses. I think the two go together.'

Another link between Toronto and Alpha was noted by Alan Morrison in an *Evangelical Times* article in November 1994. Alan Morrison wrote:

'The Airport Church in Toronto has... become the focus of international attention as church leaders from all over the world have attended there and "brought back" the phenomena to their own churches. In the UK the first recipients were the Anglican Holy Trinity Brompton... But there is another major contributing influence, which has been working among the churches today. One of the main harbingers of the "Toronto Experience" in the UK is an evangelistic ministry known as the Alpha course, a ten-week [as it was then] series of meetings first devised at Holy Trinity Brompton in 1977 and now overseen by Nicky Gumbel, curate of the Kensington Church... the acclaimed climax of the course is what is known as "the Holy Spirit weekend"... a residential weekend during which the participants receive teaching in talks entitled *What does the Holy Spirit do?* and *How can I be filled with the Holy Spirit?* It is during this weekend that unusual phenomena are expected to occur... Nicky Gumbel says that "For most people the weekend is the crucial turning-point. There are more people converted at the Alpha weekend than at any other time."'

Alan Morrison astutely added 'But what is it they are converted to?' We will consider that issue later!

So much for Nicky Gumbel and Toronto but what about Sandy Millar and Toronto? A report in the *Evangelical Times* of September 1994 highlighted the role of Sandy Millar in the distribution of 'Toronto'. The report stated:

'People from all over the world are flocking to a small building a hundred yards from the end of the runway of Toronto airport... every night there are astounding scenes of people shaking with laughter, slipping into a trance, falling to the floor and crying... Back in the UK members of Holy Trinity Brompton have been undergoing similar experiences... The vicar, Sandy Millar reminded us of the "strange things that had happened the previous Sunday" and requested witnesses to step forward to recount their experiences. A young man duly came forward and told of the ecstatic sensations he had had the previous week after Mr Millar had touched him and he had fallen to the floor... "Shall we try it again?" asked Mr Millar. The man assented. Mr Millar prayed. We held our breath. Mr Millar touched the man's forehead and then bam! Right on cue, his eyelids fluttered, his knees buckled and he was lowered to the floor where he started to gibber. Soon there were four bodies on the floor; two giggling, one gibbering and one silent. Then the curates began praying and touching the congregation, which was now falling about me.'

On 29 April 1995 I spoke at a Church in Glasgow on the subject of the 'Toronto Blessing'. When the meeting was over two young men and a girl spoke to me. They had just been to a large Christian gathering held at Wunderwest (Butlins near Ayr), and Sandy Millar had been one of the speakers.

He had 'laid hands' on two teenage girls from Northern Ireland to impart 'The Blessing' and one of them supposedly received 'the gift of tongues'. Later, in the middle of the night, this young girl was discovered by her friend rolling on the floor with staring eyes.

Her condition was so bad that next day her parents from Templepatrick had to come over and take her home. In the words of the girl herself and her friends she 'believed she received something evil'. Certainly it was 'no blessing'.

Toronto, tongues and Alpha would, in the words of a well-known expression, appear to be 'inextricably linked'. In a report in the *Daily Telegraph* of 22 December 1990, Damian Thompson wrote:

> 'Caroline, a 28 year old Cambridge graduate, was taken to Holy Trinity Brompton by a friend who

> claimed it had changed his life. Within weeks she was put on an Alpha course... culminating in a weekend in Malshanger, a country house near Basingstoke, Hampshire. It was there she experienced doubts – "I felt my emotions were being manipulated" she says. "People would say – 'we need lots of tissues for this song' – as if every tear was carefully calculated." "Speaking in tongues" was de rigueur [necessary]. "They insisted so I made a silly noise. Everyone hugged and kissed me."'

It is my view that any pastor, preacher or Bible teacher who embraced, received and passed on the 'Toronto Blessing' and who believed and who still believes that 'Toronto' was a move of the Holy Spirit should not be entrusted with the solemn task of teaching the Word of God, for they are not, in the words of Paul to Timothy 'faithful men'. In the light of what you have just heard – I ask – are Nicky Gumbel and Sandy Millar 'faithful men'?

How the men of Alpha react to 'false gospels'

Another legitimate test I believe of whether or not Bible teachers are 'faithful men' – men to whom the task of teaching the Word of God can be entrusted – is to look at their reaction to obvious 'false gospels', whether those 'false gospels' claim to be Christian or non-Christian.

Roman Catholicism clearly presents a 'false gospel' and so 'faithful men' should confront it – not cooperate with it. Is that how the 'men of Alpha' react to Roman Catholicism? In what was a locally produced ecumenical/charismatic magazine called *Bread* the following report was published in March 1996.

> 'The first Ireland Alpha conference was held in St Patrick's College [A Roman Catholic college] Drumcondra on the 30th November and 1st December 1995. Speakers at the conference included Sandy Millar, vicar of Holy Trinity Brompton, London... Alpha courses have been

organised in Catholic and Protestant parishes in Ireland, both north and south... Charles Whitehead of International Catholic Charismatic Services said "Alpha is an excellent introductory course for those who do not go to church or for whom an inherited Christianity has little meaning."'

So much for Sandy Millar and Roman Catholicism – but what about Nicky Gumbel? The *Irish Catholic* newspaper of 10 September 1998 printed an article called *A Way To Grow The Church* – let me quote:

'Last weekend St Patrick's College, Drumcondra, hosted a conference on a new evangelisation course gaining in popularity worldwide... Nicky Gumbel, one of those who developed the Alpha course addressed the audience attending the Alpha conference... Gerard Gallagher explains how the Alpha programme works and how he is using it to develop the faith of the young adults in Ireland... "Through Alpha I have witnessed young adults who have taken on new understandings of Christianity... Alpha is only a vehicle to be used. Follow up is essential... It is recommended that Alpha only be used within one denomination. Co-hosting it with other Christian faiths is not recommended as it only causes confusion."'

That Roman Catholic article mentioned the importance of 'follow up'. On the front page of *Alpha News* (July – October 1999), is a large colour photograph of 'Father' Raniero Cantalamessa and a smaller inset photo of him with Nicky Gumbel. Below these photos is written:

'Father Raniero Cantalamessa, the Preacher to the Papal Household in the Vatican has accepted an invitation from *the catholic Alpha office* to give a series of seven talks on video which will be used as follow up teaching to Alpha in the Roman Catholic Church. The series entitled, "Drink From The Wells Of The Church" [not from The Word of God!] includes talks on the Bible, Prayer, The Church and The Power of Pentecost... David Payne, head of *the UK Catholic Alpha office* said, "These videos have just been published and we are very excited about their potential."'

This little write-up in *Alpha News* failed to mention other titles in the video series such as 'The Eucharist Makes Us Holy' and 'Mary Our Model'. The reality is that Alpha is nothing more than an 'anorexic skeleton' of supposed Christianity which Rome then, in her video series, 'fleshes out' with all its unscriptural, soul-damning heresies.

On 17 June 2003, 'Father' Cantalamessa in his Vatican 'sermon' spoke on 'The Trinity' and said:

'For a believer, the Trinity is a mystery that is very familiar... Christian life, which begins with baptism in the name of The Father, of The Son and of The Holy Spirit develops submerged in the Trinitarian dimension, whether in confirmation, or in the sacrament of marriage or at the hour of death.'

Would you invite such a man to come and teach Christianity in your Church? Well, that's precisely what Holy Trinity Brompton did in the summer of 2003. According to a report in the *British Church Newspaper* of 9 January 2004:

'In July 2003, Preacher to the Papal Household, "Father" Raniero Cantalamessa made an extended visit to Holy Trinity Brompton, headquarters of the Alpha movement... Cantalamessa's sermon to young people at Holy Trinity's "Home Focus Week" exalted *Mary* not *Christ* as "our hope and model."'

The report went on to say:

'Cantalamessa is closely involved with the international development of the Alpha course. The Papacy now has its own Alpha office. Roman

Catholic Archbishop Ambrose Griffiths recently
described Alpha as "The most powerful
evangelistic tool which reaches out to those
whom we need."'

In his talks, Nicky Gumbel regularly refers favourably to, and
quotes favourably from, people who were or are faithful,
practising Roman Catholics – people like Mother Teresa,
Malcolm Muggeridge and Hans Kung.

Hans Kung, a controversial Roman Catholic theologian stated:

'No world peace without peace among the
religions.'

And of course that's the popular view today amongst those
human beings 'with clout' in the corridors of political and
religious world power. As well as these Roman Catholics Nicky
Gumbel also made favourable references to:

- C S Lewis, who believed in 'Purgatory' and 'salvation'
  apart from Christ.

- William Temple, former Archbishop of Canterbury and
  President of the World Council of Churches, who,
  according to author Edward Panosian 'found rays of the
  same light which shone forth in Christ also in non-
  Christian religions'.

- William Barclay, described by Martyn Lloyd-Jones as
  'the most dangerous man in Christendom'.

- John Wimber, Ecumenical/Charismatic founder of 'The
  Vineyard Movement' that in 1994 spawned the so-
  called 'Toronto Blessing'.

There is an upsurge of opinion in 'professing Christendom'
today – both Catholic and Protestant – that there is hope for
those who have never heard of Christ. Rome teaches it; Billy
Graham teaches it; Clark Pinnock of 'Open Theism' infamy
teaches it. This 'hope' can either be through 'natural reasoning'
or 'God's wider mercy'.

To the list of those who hold out hope for those who have never heard of Christ you can add the name of Nicky Gumbel. Here are extracts from an article in *Evangelical Times* of August 2002 by Norman Mackay that critiques a book written by Nicky Gumbel called *What About Other Religions?* – according to the article this book is referred to as 'An Alpha Resource'. Norman Mackay writes:

> 'The booklet seeks to tackle issues arising from the interaction of Christians with those of other faiths. Two questions are raised in the booklet. [1] Is Jesus the only way to God? [2] What about those who have never heard of Christ? Are they eternally lost? To the first question the booklet answers in the affirmative. Yet regarding the second we are told that many who do not hear of Christ are likely to be saved anyway.'

In short this Alpha Resource unashamedly endorses what has come to be known as the 'wider hope' theory. The 'wider hope' theory is grounded on the assertion that people can be saved by virtue of Christ's death without ever consciously hearing of him or embracing the Good News concerning him. Rather than seeing the world as a harvest field of unreached peoples, we are led to believe that the planet is populated by millions of 'anonymous Christians'. These people are going about their business as Muslims, Buddhists, Hindus and animists, totally oblivious of the person and work of Christ, yet are actually saved by Christ. The question is whether these incredible claims can actually be true. If what Nicky Gumbel's book teaches was actually true, then why did the Apostle Paul apparently waste his time and energy writing these words in Romans 10:12-15?

> 'For there is no difference between the Jew and the Greek: for the same Lord over all is rich unto all that call upon him. For whosoever shall call upon the name of the Lord shall be saved. How then shall they call on him in whom they have not believed? and how shall they believe in him of whom they have not heard? and how shall they

> hear without a preacher? And how shall they
> preach, except they be sent? as it is written, How
> beautiful are the feet of them that preach the gospel
> of peace, and bring glad tidings of good things!'

As well as this 'wider hope' theory, many who subscribe to it, also subscribe to a 'natural reasoning' hope of salvation for those who have never heard of Christ.

God's Word demolished any notion of 'salvation through natural reasoning' when Paul wrote in 1 Corinthians 1:21 that 'in the wisdom of God, the world by wisdom knew not God'. When it comes to a link between 'reasoning' and 'salvation' there must be an input of 'divine truth' – for Paul continued to say 'it pleased God by the foolishness of *preaching* [divine input] to save them that believe'. Even in the Old Testament God said in Isaiah 1:18 'Come now and let *us* [a divine input] reason together'.

As for God supposedly extending 'wider mercy' to those who practise non-Christian faiths, Romans 1:18 tells us that God does not 'reveal His mercy' to such people but rather 'His wrath'.

As was the case in the matter of the 'Toronto Blessing' it is again my view that any pastor, preacher or Bible teacher who cooperates with Rome rather than confronting Rome and who holds out hope of salvation to those who never hear of Christ: such a person, and Nicky Gumbel is one such person, should not be entrusted with teaching the Word of God, for he and they are not, in Paul's words to Timothy 'faithful men'.

So much for 'the men of Alpha', but what about 'the message of Alpha'?

The message of Alpha

As we come to consider this I want to quote from Acts chapter 20 as Paul is saying farewell to the Elders of the Church at Ephesus:

> 'And now, behold, I know that ye all, among
> whom I have gone preaching the kingdom of God,
> shall see my face no more. Wherefore I take you to

record this day, that I am pure from the blood of all
men. For I have not shunned to declare unto you
all the counsel of God. Take heed therefore unto
yourselves, and to all the flock, over the which the
Holy Ghost hath made you overseers, to feed the
church of God, which he hath purchased with his
own blood.' (Acts 20:25-28)

As we continue to assess Alpha the question must be asked:
'Does Alpha declare all the counsel of God?' Are all the *vital*
and *crucial* elements that make up '*all* the counsel of God'
included in it? When I'm asked what I think of Alpha, I very
often reply by saying: 'The Church of Rome endorses it, need I
say more?'

Any Bible course that Rome is able to endorse cannot possibly
be 'Evangelizing the Lost' or 'Equipping the Saints'. But there
are other deficiencies where Alpha is concerned and I want to
look at them now.

The 'God' that Paul spoke of as he addressed the elders at
Ephesus is of course the 'Triune God' of Father, Son and Holy
Spirit revealed to us in the inspired Scriptures. I believe that
'The message of Alpha' fails to 'declare all the counsel' of God
The Father, of God The Son and of God The Holy Spirit.

In relation to The Father, I believe Alpha fails to adequately
declare His *Majesty* – majesty is defined as 'stateliness' or
'nobility'. When Isaiah had his vision of heaven we read:

'In the year that king Uzziah died I saw also the
Lord sitting upon a throne, high and lifted up, and
his train filled the temple. Above it stood the
seraphims... And one cried unto another, and
said, Holy, holy, holy, is the LORD of hosts: the
whole earth is full of his glory.' (Isaiah 6:1-3)

The 'stateliness', the 'nobility', the 'majesty', that which brings
'glory' to The Father 'upon the whole earth' is 'His Holiness'.
When the Lord was praying in John 17, He addressed His Father
as 'Holy Father' in verse 11. This 'Holiness' has crucial and

vital ramifications or consequences. A W Pink, on pages 43-45 of his book *The Attributes of God*, wrote:

> 'Because God is holy He hates all sin. He loves everything which is conformity to His law and loathes everything which is contrary to it... It follows therefore that He must necessarily punish sin... God has often forgiven sinners but He never forgives sin; and the sinner is only forgiven on the ground of Another having borne his punishment... For one sin God banished our first parents from Eden... The unregenerate do not really believe in the holiness of God. Their conception of His character is altogether one-sided... The "god" which the vast majority of professing Christians "love" is looked upon very much like an indulgent old man, who himself has no relish for "folly" but leniently winks at the "indiscretion" of youth. But the Word says "Thou hatest all workers of iniquity" [Psalm 5:5]; "God is angry with the wicked every day" [Psalm 7:11]... Because God is holy, we should desire to be conformed to Him. His command is "Be ye holy, for I am holy" [1 Peter 1:16].'

Back in 1869, C H Spurgeon, that 'prince of preachers' said:

> 'In holiness God is more clearly seen than in anything else, save in the person of Christ Jesus the Lord, of whose life such holiness is but a repetition.'

To grasp something of the *majesty* or the *holiness* of 'The Father' A W Pink drew attention to something vital and crucial to the process of our understanding of 'The Father' – he referred to 'His law'. If men are ever to appreciate 'God's Holiness' and their own lack of it, they need to be confronted with 'God's Law'.

Chris Hand, in his book *Falling Short*, writes of:

> '...a failure to teach God's holiness. This is
> extraordinary given the fact that "God is holy" is
> taught far more often in scripture than "God is
> love". Indeed the adjective used most frequently
> in scripture to describe God is "holy."'

Tim Chapman (an Anglican curate) wrote a helpful article entitled
The Alpha Course Examined, and on this point he wrote:

> 'Alpha is intended to be a presentation of the
> gospel that will bring people to faith... the Alpha
> material posits [lays down as a principle] that
> people are best brought to faith without God's
> holiness and sovereign rule over the world being
> taught. The consequences of such a diminished
> definition of the character of God are enormous.
> Nowhere is this more clearly seen than in Alpha's
> treatment of sin. Alpha is clear to begin with on
> what is at the heart of sin when it states that the
> "root cause of sin is a broken relationship with
> God". The consequences of sin are spelt out in
> terms of the pollution, the power, the penalty and
> partition of sin.
>
> But then as the argument in the course is
> followed, sin is presented as being "the mess we
> make of our own lives". The problem of sin is
> explained as "the rubbish that clutters up our lives
> and clutters up our world" and as "pollution of
> the soul". For all its biblical use of words, Alpha
> fails to define sin biblically. It does so by
> concentrating on the consequences of sin rather
> than on what sin actually is.'

I witnessed this failure 'to define sin biblically' at first hand
when I went to hear an Alpha presentation at the Waterfront
Hall in Belfast on 25 September 2000. The speaker was Nicky
Gumbel and in a report that I wrote I said this:

'The whole thrust of Nicky Gumbel's message focussed upon man and his problems – there was nothing said about the world and mankind as seen from God's perspective... God's love was mentioned frequently but "the fierceness of his anger" [Joshua 7:26] never got a mention. As a result there was no attempt to induce "reverent fear" of the Lord, which is of course the beginning of true "knowledge" [Proverbs 1:7]... There was studiously no reference to or use of the word "sin"... Man's problems were identified as "wrongdoings" but never was any yardstick identified in the... light of which man's actions could be classified as "wrongdoings" [in other words there was no mention of God's law, which of course is "the schoolmaster" ordained "to bring us unto Christ" (Galatians 3:24)].'

as an afterthought I could add Romans 3:20 where Paul wrote: 'by the law is the knowledge of sin'.

C H Spurgeon said, around 1886:

'I do not believe that any man can preach the gospel who does not preach the law. The law is the needle, and you cannot draw the silken thread of the gospel through a man's heart unless you first send the needle of the law to make way for it. If men do not understand the law they will not feel that they are sinners. And if they are not consciously sinners, they will never value the sin offering. There is no healing a man till the law has wounded him, no making him alive till the law has slain him.'

Tim Chapman wrote of how Alpha was 'concentrating on the consequences of sin rather than on what sin actually is' and in Belfast that was the thrust of Nicky Gumbel's message. He basically took the audience on a 'pity-party guilt trip' where he focused on man's 'wrongdoings' and the resultant 'plight' and 'miseries'. Not once, in my hearing did Nicky Gumbel spell out the 'Divine Consequences' of man's 'wrongdoings' – of how God's Holiness is offended and His wrath incurred.

In a book called *Straight Talks* by Thomas Fitch, published in 1950, Mr Fitch in his preface wrote:

> 'The short addresses which comprise this volume were all delivered to Service personnel while I was on active service as a chaplain in the Army.'

One of these 'addresses' was entitled *Repentance* and in it [p34-36] Mr Fitch wrote:

> 'If we were to ask the question "What is repentance?" we would discover by a close investigation that there are many parts which combine to make up the whole... First then, confession. Confession is part of repentance but before there can be confession there must be conviction of sin, otherwise no need of confession is felt... Second, contrition. This is another part of the content of repentance. Let me point out that there is what is theologically known as *attrition* as well as *contrition* and these two require to be carefully distinguished. *Attrition* is simply sorrow because of the consequences of sin. *Contrition* is sorrow *for* sin. Sorrow that is aroused because the sin hurts another... The sinner, aware of his sin in no small way, becomes truly sorry for that which hurts the heart of God... An apology to gain an immediate advantage must never on any account be considered as true contrition.'

In Belfast Nicky Gumbel was certainly seeking to induce *attrition* in the hearts of his listeners but to the exclusion of *contrition*.

Such an approach, an approach central to 'The Message of Alpha' 'shuns to declare' the *majesty* of God The Father.

Then, in relation to The Son I believe Alpha fails to adequately declare His *Mission*: What was the mission of God the Son? The angel said to Joseph in Matthew 1:21 'thou shalt call his name JESUS: for he shall save his people from their sins'. The Apostle Paul wrote in 1 Timothy 1:15 'This is a faithful saying, and worthy of all acceptation, that Christ Jesus came into the world to save sinners'.

We've all heard the three-fold explanation of how Christ saves people from sin: [1] From its *penalty* – by His dying as a substitute for sinners at Calvary, believing sinners can be 'justified' – totally pardoned from the *penalty* of sin. Then [2] Christ saves from sin's *power* – in the lives of believers, God, through the work and influence of the Holy Spirit 'sanctifies' His people, or as Charles Wesley wrote so well 'He breaks the power of cancelled sin'. Then [3] Christ will, when believers get to heaven, 'glorify' them by saving them from the *presence* of sin.

That was the 'saving' *mission* of God the Son.

Chris Hand in *Falling Short* wrote:

> 'The consequences of sin are true enough. But it is all man centred... Alpha's emphasis does not go anything like far enough. Christ in Alpha, comes forward to deal with too small a problem... sin according to Alpha is more of a problem for us than it is for God... the misunderstanding of sin inevitably leads to a misunderstanding of the cross.'

Tim Chapman, in his article, wrote:

> 'Alpha gets off to a good start. After seeking to establish "Who is Jesus?" the session "Why did Jesus die?" tells us that "the cross lies at the heart of the Christian faith" (Alpha Manual page 10). We are told that the cross achieved justification, redemption, atonement and reconciliation and scripture references are provided. Indeed there is a reasonable foundation to build on if one wanted to further investigate the Cross.

However the penal substitutionary nature of Christ's atonement is given very little weight – that Christ died not simply in our place but took upon himself the wrath of God against sin. It is skimmed over in the course. This is hardly surprising given that there is an incorrect view of the disease of sin in Alpha; the cure of the cross is similarly misrepresented. We are left with a hollow view of why Jesus had to die at all. Thus the cross ends up being little more than a visual aid, which proves that God is self-sacrificial and loving. The death of Jesus is presented as being an act of love yet without any connection with the reality of God's holy anger. This is a far cry from the biblical teaching on the atonement.'

In my own report of my visit to the Waterfront Hall I wrote:

'Jesus was presented as one who would be able to "satisfy" people... The answer to what was being put across as... man's "pity party" is, according to Nicky Gumbel, friendship and companionship with God. Whilst that is in part true... Friendship was elevated and exalted above forgiveness as being the means to happiness for man... The real answer to happiness, with an ensuing friendship and companionship with God, is found in Psalm 32:1 "Blessed is he whose transgression is forgiven, whose sin is covered."'

The 'Jesus' of Alpha is portrayed more as a 'Solver of human problems' rather than as a 'Saviour from sin'. He comes across like a spiritual 'Jim'll fix it' character rather than 'The Good Shepherd who gave His life for His sheep'. He is presented as One who rescues people from the consequences of their 'wrongdoings' rather than as One who redeems people from the condemnation of their 'sins'. I think Alpha's Jesus would appeal to former soccer idol, George Best, with all his alcohol problems, but the Biblical Jesus would not – unless of course the Spirit of God did a dealing with him.

Alpha, by failing in the first place to adequately 'declare all the counsel of God' concerning the *majesty* of God The Father, fails secondly to adequately 'declare all the counsel of God' concerning the *mission* of God The Son.

Then thirdly, in relation to The Holy Spirit I believe Alpha fails to adequately declare His *Ministry*. What was to be the *ministry* of God the Holy Spirit?

The Lord Jesus Himself identified it in John's Gospel and there would clearly be two aspects to the Holy Spirit's ministry. The first applies to unbelievers, when the Lord said in John 16:8-11,

> 'And when he is come, he will reprove the world of sin, and of righteousness, and of judgment: Of sin, because they believe not on me; Of righteousness, because I go to my Father, and ye see me no more; Of judgment, because the prince of this world is judged.'

Matthew Henry wrote:

> 'Convincing work is the Spirit's work; he can do it effectually, and none but he. It is the method the Holy Spirit takes, first to convince, and then to comfort. The Spirit shall convince the world, of sin; not merely tell them of it. The Spirit convinces of the fact of sin; of the fault of sin; of the folly of sin; of the filth of sin, that by it we are become hateful to God; of the fountain of sin, the corrupt nature; and lastly, of the fruit of sin, that the end thereof is death. The Holy Spirit proves that all the world is guilty before God. He convinces the world of righteousness; that Jesus of Nazareth was Christ the righteous. Also, of Christ's righteousness, imparted to us for justification and salvation. He will show them where it is to be had, and how they may be accepted as righteous in God's sight.'

There we have the Holy Spirit's ministry to unbelievers clearly spelt out by the Lord Himself. But the Lord also identified what the Holy Spirit's ministry to believers would be. In John 14:26 He said:

> 'But the Comforter, which is the Holy Ghost, whom the Father will send in my name, he shall teach you all things, and bring all things to your remembrance, whatsoever I have said unto you.'

Then in John 16:13-15 the Lord also said:

> 'Howbeit when he, the Spirit of truth, is come, he will guide you into all truth: for he shall not speak of himself; but whatsoever he shall hear, that shall he speak: and he will shew you things to come. He shall glorify me: for he shall receive of mine, and shall shew it unto you. All things that the Father hath are mine: therefore said I, that he shall take of mine, and shall shew it unto you.'

So, to summarise, the ministry of the Holy Spirit to unbelievers is to *convict of sin* and to *convert to Christ*.

His ministry to believers is to *teach* and to *transform*.

And overall his ministry, which again has at its heart the issue of 'sin' – the revealing of sin's 'penalty' to unbelievers and the removal of sin's 'power' in the lives of believers – *that ministry should not draw attention to the Holy Spirit, but should glorify Christ.*

I believe Alpha fails to adequately declare this ministry.

Tim Chapman, in his article *The Alpha Course Examined*, wrote in relation to what the Lord said in John chapters 14-17:

> 'These chapters teach us that there is an indissoluble connection between the word of God and the Spirit of God, a connection which runs right through Scripture... Given what Jesus teaches about His Holy Spirit we should expect Him [the Holy Spirit] to point towards Jesus and His words and not to himself.'

Earlier in his article Tim Chapman wrote:

> 'I would suggest that too much of the limited time in what is an evangelistic course is spent on the subject of the Holy Spirit... In the talk "How can I be filled with the Holy Spirit?", the fullness of the spirit is presented as a subsequent experience to conversion... There is scant evidence in scripture to suggest anything other than that the believer receives all of the Holy Spirit when he or she repents, puts their trust in Jesus and is justified. "Be being filled with the spirit" in Ephesians 5:18 is an ongoing command which acknowledges variation in filling among Christians but not a requirement to seek a second filling. The teaching "Every Christian has the Holy Spirit, but not every Christian is filled with the Spirit" (Alpha manual, HTB Publishing, page 33) is at odds with Biblical teaching.'

Not only is Alpha's teaching on the ministry of the Holy Spirit 'inadequate' but it is also positively 'unscriptural'. Paul's command in Ephesians 5:18 to 'Be filled with the Holy Spirit' was given to *believers* who were already indwelt by the Holy Spirit in all His fullness – The Spirit was God's gracious gift to them at the moment of their conversion and He still is today. But this is not how Alpha portrays the 'fullness of the spirit'. For Alpha this can be an experience for *unbelievers*.

Tim Chapman rightly identified this 'unscriptural' misrepresentation when he wrote:

> 'Gumbel's reasoning suggests that there are two equally valid ways of becoming a Christian; one is to be persuaded by rational and historical explanations, and the other is by experiencing the Holy Spirit. To think thus is to ignore the fact that it is always the apostles' priority to present rational and historical explanations to all sorts of people wherever they proclaimed the gospel. It is the Holy Spirit who then applies these words to

people's hearts and convicts them of their sin.
This [Holy Spirit weekend] appears to be yet
another way that the apostolic gospel is bypassed
in an effort to make things as accessible as
possible... For many the decisive moment is the
Saturday evening of the weekend... For Alpha
the decisive moment is not the preaching of
Christ and Him crucified, but when the Holy
Spirit is 'invoked'... Surely the moment when the
guest repents and believes must be the decisive
moment.'

Friends, we must never forget that the Holy Trinity Brompton
church and its leaders Sandy Millar and Nicky Gumbel were
'infected by' and 'carriers of' the diabolical so-called 'Toronto
Blessing' and they clearly believe that if they can introduce
people to similar 'Toronto-Type' experiences then that for them
equates to that person becoming a Christian!

ITV broadcast a series of programmes that showed the
experiences of a group of people who 'signed up' for an Alpha
course. When it came to week four – 'The Holy Spirit
Weekend' – none of them had professed to having become a
Christian, yet here they were on their way to a 'weekend' where
they were hoping to 'be filled with the Holy Spirit'.

TV cameras were only allowed to show Nicky Gumbel
explaining this to the gathering of several hundred people –
most of whom would not have been believers. When it came to
the point where he was going to 'pray down the spirit' the
cameras had to leave. Friends, this is not 'scriptural' this is
'spiritism' and the testimonies of people afterwards prove it.

Several of the group who were the subject of the TV series were
interviewed as they left this particular meeting and for many it
had been either a time of terror or of shock or both. Not only
were they frightened but they were angry and there was
certainly no mention on their lips of the glories of Christ or
Calvary.

Tim Chapman wrote:

> 'On the Alpha leaders tapes there is a peculiar mystique about giving the talk "How can I be filled with the Holy Spirit?" Both Sandy Millar when talking of his conversion and Nicky Gumbel when talking of his giving this talk give a consistent message, that the Holy Spirit weekend is the highlight of Alpha. Yet isn't this teaching both to demean the Holy Spirit and to misunderstand his work... Moreover if the Spirit's longing is to point to Christ and to bring Him the glory then isn't it strange that Christ is so infrequently mentioned?'

In some instances the Holy Spirit has been put across as a 'passport to party-time'. Gerald Coates, one of the co-founders of 'Marches For Jesus' and director of the 'Pioneer' group of charismatic churches said:

> 'Alpha courses have been successfully used among our Pioneer network of churches... The course is fun and unthreatening – just like our Lord Himself.'

The Lord – 'fun and unthreatening'?

Try telling that to those who witnessed Him with a whip driving out the corrupt money changers from the Temple in John 2:15.

Try telling that to 'the goats' who according to Matthew 25:41 will be consigned to 'everlasting fire' by this 'unthreatening' Lord.

Gerald Coates is not alone in portraying the Holy Spirit as a 'conduit to celebrations'. Elizabeth McDonald, in her little booklet *Alpha New Life or New Lifestyle?*, has a section on page 20 entitled *The Parable of The Party*. Elizabeth writes:

> 'In Section IV, Gumbel says the Church, though God's Holy Temple, so often loses "the sense of the presence of God in its midst". He is making reference here to the Sunday meetings of

believers rather than to the Church as the body of Christ and uses the parable of the Prodigal Son to explain that Sunday services should be like a "party". "Jesus was saying that… the Church is like… a feast and a celebration and at a party everyone has a good time. There's fun, there's laughter… Why shouldn't there be laughter at the biggest party of all? And that's what we're seeing today, laughter and fun and people getting drunk – not with wine, Paul says 'don't get drunk with wine – be filled with the Spirit'…Come to a party where you can get drunk on God… I was at a party like that last night. It was a whole load of church leaders, and we invited the Spirit to come… It was a party thrown by the Holy Spirit… It was a fun place to be. The Church is meant to be a party… That's the sort of picture – a Holy Temple."'

'The message of Alpha' shuns to declare the *majesty* of God the Father.

'The message of Alpha' shuns to declare the *mission* of God the Son.

'The message of Alpha' shuns to declare the *ministry* of God the Holy Spirit.

This failure where Alpha is concerned is due to what I would call 'The Missing Link' – the missing link in Alpha is its failure to address *the seriousness of sin*.

They do not adequately explain the Father's *view* of sin.

They do not adequately explain the Son's *redemption* from sin.

They do not adequately explain the Holy Spirit's *conviction* of sin.

Earlier I made the comment:

> 'When I'm asked what I think of Alpha – I very often reply by saying "The Church of Rome endorses it – need I say more?"'

Perhaps this should not be a surprise for the truth is that Rome does not adequately explain the Father's *view* of sin. Rome categorizes 'sin' as either 'venial' or 'mortal'.

Rome does not adequately explain the Son's *redemption* from sin. Rome introduces concepts of 'eternal' and 'temporal' punishment.

Rome does not adequately explain the Holy Spirit's *conviction* of sin. Rome teaches that the Holy Spirit uses baptismal water, and miraculously transubstantiated bread and wine, in the hands of her consecrated priests, to deal with sin.

Alpha and Rome have a shared 'missing link'. Together they minimize and misrepresent *the seriousness of sin*.

As we come to our final assessment on Alpha I want to quote some verses from Matthew 7:15-18,

> 'Beware of false prophets, which come to you in sheep's clothing, but inwardly they are ravening wolves. Ye shall know them by their fruits. Do men gather grapes of thorns, or figs of thistles? Even so every good tree bringeth forth good fruit; but a corrupt tree bringeth forth evil fruit. A good tree cannot bring forth evil fruit, neither can a corrupt tree bring forth good fruit.'

Commenting on this passage, Bishop J C Ryle wrote:

> 'We must beware of false prophets. They will arise... we must be prepared for them and on our guard... There are thousands who seem ready to believe anything in religion if they hear it from an ordained minister... Their teaching must be weighed in the balance of Holy Scripture...

Sound doctrine and holy living are the marks of true prophets.'

If 'teaching' is false then any resultant fruit from that 'false teaching' cannot, according to this passage be 'good' but will be 'evil'. Am I saying that no one who attends an Alpha course can be 'saved'? – No I'm not. God is sovereign and if someone is genuinely saved whilst attending an Alpha course then it will be in spite of the course and not because of it. But that doesn't allow us to endorse Alpha. Paul in Romans 3:8 had to deny a charge that he was teaching that it was legitimate to 'do evil that good may come' and for us to endorse Alpha would be to 'do evil that good may come'.

The question must be faced up to:

Can an 'evangelistic course' that minimizes and misrepresents *the seriousness of sin* really produce 'good fruit'?

Tim Chapman wrote:

> 'The lack of focus on Jesus is seen very clearly in the testimonies people give – testimonies which Alpha quotes with approval in its literature.'

Referring to various 'testimonies' Tim Chapman continues:

> 'This is deeply troubling... The focus of his attention is specifically identified as being not the Lord Jesus, not the Cross but the third session "How can I be filled with the Spirit?" Sadly such a testimony is repeated again and again. This is hardly surprising, as guests are made expectant of variously; "physical heat sometimes accompanies the filling of the Spirit and people experience it in their hands or some other part of their bodies". The experience is described as "glowing all over, liquid heat, burning in my arms when I was not hot". Still another said "I didn't want to come to the weekend and I did. But I would call myself a Christian now. I would say that I felt the Holy

Spirit. I was feeling I was loved. It was really a tremendous overwhelming feeling of love". Again what is conspicuous by its absence in so many of these testimonies is any mention of Jesus and his atoning sacrifice on the Cross, which is the heart of the Biblical gospel.'

When I spoke publicly on Alpha in 2000, I made exactly this same point and I cited several examples. I mentioned the TV presenter Diane Louise Jordan. In the March – July 2000 *Alpha News* there were three pages devoted to her 'testimony'. In those three pages there was not one reference to *sin*, *Christ* or *Calvary*. The major influences in her 'claimed conversion' were her emotional reaction to a visit to Lourdes and an encounter with an apparition of her dead sister in a hotel room in Argentina.

Since then, in the March – June 2003 *Alpha News* in two pages of 'testimony' by former female spiritualist Sam Ryan, yet again there was no reference to either *sin* or *Calvary*. In the July – October 2003 *Alpha News* in two pages of 'testimony' Leila Bagnall makes no reference to *Calvary*.

Disgraced MP, Jonathan Aitken refers to his 'conversion' in these terms, as apparently someone was praying for the Holy Spirit to descend on him:

'I obeyed his instructions to stand with hands outstretched at waist height, palms upwards, praying that the Holy Spirit would come... At this point my palms suddenly began to tingle with a strange physical sensation which strengthened until my hands and wrists became hot and uncomfortable as though they were being charged with an electric current. Then I began to cry.'

Other apparent claimed Alpha converts would include former spice-girl Gerri Halliwell and page three topless model Samantha Fox. The life-styles of these two ladies since their claimed 'conversions' would place lots of questions marks over the validity of Alpha's claim that they 'came to faith'. A 'convert' in the TV series – when asked what he had been 'saved' from – answered by saying 'from the way he used to live'. He had embraced a 'new life-style' – but had he received 'eternal life'?

From the 'Tree of Alpha' one can pick a large basket of 'questionable testimonies'.

From the 'Tree of Alpha' one can also pick a large basket of 'dubious endorsers'.

People are often known by 'the company they keep'. In the November 1996 *Alpha News*, several pages were devoted to 'endorsements' from what were described as 'Church Leaders and Evangelists'. Amongst those listed were:

- Gerald Coates and Roger Forster, charismatic joint founders of 'Marches for Jesus'.

- Ken Gott, head of a charismatic centre in Sunderland who was smitten by the 'Toronto Blessing'.

- Steve Chalke, who called for 'street parties' when Princess Diana died. In a review [in *Evangelicals Now* – June 2004] by Andrew Sach and Mike Ovey of Steve Chalke's book *The Lost Message of Jesus* we read the following:

  > 'If God is not angry and humans are not essentially guilty, then what job remains for the cross? Unsurprisingly, Chalke renounces a crucial biblical dimension of the atonement: penal substitution. For Chalke this is unnecessary and offensive... But the apostle John declares that the pouring out of God's wrath on Jesus is the very essence of love [1 John 4:10].'

In the 20 August 2004 issue of the *British Church* newspaper we read:

  > 'Reformed commentators have heavily criticised Steve Chalke, "Evangelical" TV personality and director of Christian charity

"Oasis Trust" for his strongly expressed criticisms of the biblical doctrine of penal substitution. He has now condemned the accounts of creation in Genesis and Exodus as "rubbish"... Steve Chalke said "My personal belief is that those who wish to read into Genesis chapter 1 that God made the world in six days are not being honest and scholarly. It won't be taught in the school [a new 'Christian Academy' to be opened by Oasis trust] because I think it's rubbish. It's a bizarre thing to claim the Bible suggests that". [Comment: Does Steve Chalke not believe the fourth commandment? – "For in six days the Lord made heaven and earth" (Exodus 20:11).]'

- J John, leading 'evangelist' who was 'intoxicated by Toronto'.

- R T Kendall, former pastor of Westminster Chapel who endorsed Rodney Howard Browne.

- J I Packer and O S Guiness, endorsers of the 1994 ECT Agreement.

- Mike Bickle, founder of the so-called 'Kansas City Prophets'.

- George Carey, former Archbishop of Canterbury.

- Alpha has also consistently received endorsements from leading Roman Catholic Archbishops.

That's the sort of company that no faithful 'Child of God' would want to be seen in.

Conclusions

The real 'fruit' of Alpha:

– Questionable testimonies

– Dubious endorsers

The men of alpha – *unfaithful*

The message of Alpha – *unscriptural*

The 'fruit' of Alpha – *unconvincing*

I see no reason to change my verdict on Alpha:

the verdict that I reached in my talk in 2000,

THIS IS A COURSE TO AVOID.

Bibliography

Was C S Lewis truly 'Our greatest Christian writer'?

Andrews, Cecil. *Was C S Lewis Truly 'Our Greatest Christian Writer'?* 'News From The Front': 'Take Heed' Ministries: New Year 2003.

Bingham, Derick. *Thought For The Weekend.* Belfast Telegraph, 5 January 2002.

Bingham, Derick. *Thought For The Weekend.* Belfast Telegraph, 12 October 2002.

Bingham, Derick. *Walking With Giants.* TBF Thompson Ministries, 2002.

Bingham, Derick. *Our Greatest Christian Writer.* Life-Times Magazine, Issue No. 9: October 2002, Ambassador Productions.

Cairns, Alan. *Dictionary of Theological Terms.* Ambassador Productions, 1998.

Cairns, Alan (Ed.). *Footprints of Faith.* Ambassador Productions, 1989.

Cloud, David. *C S Lewis and Evangelicals Today.* Way of Life website 2000: <http://www.wayoflife.org/fbns/cslewisand.htm>.

Colson, Charles and Neuhaus, Richard (Joint Eds). *Evangelicals and Catholics Together: The Christian Mission for the Third Millennium,* 1994.

Doughan, David. *Who Was Tolkien?* The Tolkien Society website 2002:
<http://www.tolkiensociety.org/tolkien/biography.html>.

Edwards, Bruce L. *Assorted articles.* C S Lewis and the Inklings resources website:
<http://personal.bgsu.edu/~edwards/lewisr.html>.

Fay, Roger. *The Legacy of C S Lewis.* Evangelical Times: January 2002.

Hanegraaff, Hank. *Christianity in Crisis.* Harvest House Publishers, 1993.

Henry, Matthew. *Commentary on the Whole Bible: Volume VI.* Fleming H Revell Company, 1935.

Jeffrey, Peter. *Why Was Jesus Born?* Evangelical Times: December 2003.

Lewis, C S. *Mere Christianity.* Collins Fontana Books, 1974.

Lewis, C S. *Prayer: Letters to Malcolm.* Collins Fontana Books, 1974.

MacArthur, John. *The MacArthur Study Bible.* Word Publishing, 1997.

Murray, John. *Redemption Accomplished and Applied.* The Banner of Truth Trust, 1979.

Owen, John. *The Death of Death.* The Banner of Truth Trust, 2002.

Roberts, Patricia. *Personal letter about Edward Cooney.* 1994.

Robbins, John W. *Did C S Lewis Go To Heaven?* Trinity Foundation website 2003: <http://www.trinityfoundation.org/journal.php?id=103>.

Vine, W E; Unger, Merrill F and White Jnr, William (Joint Eds). *Vine's Complete Expository Dictionary of Old and New Testament Words.* Thomas Nelson Publishers, 1985.

Philip Yancey—'turning the grace of God into lasciviousness'?

Booksellers, Christian. *Registration Leaflet for UK Delegates.* Doncaster, 2002.

Chellew-Hodge, Candace (Ed.). *Assorted articles.* 'WHOSOEVER': 'An online magazine for Gay, Lesbian, Bisexual and Transgender Christians': <http://www.whosoever.org/index.shtml>.

Elwell, Walter A (Ed.). *Evangelical Dictionary of Theology.* Marshall Pickering, 1985.

Gilley, Gary. *Review of 'What's So Amazing About Grace?'* Listed on Southern View Chapel, Springfield, Illinois website, August 2003: <http://www.svchapel.org/ThinkOnTheseThingsMinistries/book reviews/book_reviews.html>.

Henry, Matthew. *Commentary on the Whole Bible: Volume VI.* Fleming H Revell Company, 1935.

Hole, F B. *Epistles (Volume Three) Hebrews – Revelation.* Central Bible Hammond Trust, Northumberland: Undated.

Metropolitan, Community Church. *Assorted articles.* MCC website, 2004: <http://www.mccchurch.org/>.

MacArthur, John. *The MacArthur Study Bible.* Word Publishing, 1997.

McCreary, Alf. *Soul Survivors.* Belfast Telegraph, 21 September 2002.

McCullough, Mona. *Personal Letter on 'What's So Amazing about Grace?'* June 2001.

Vine, W E; Unger, Merrill F and White Jnr, William (Joint Eds). *Vine's Complete Expository Dictionary of Old and New Testament Words.* Thomas Nelson Publishers, 1985.

Alpha—Attend or Avoid?

Alpha. *What Church Leaders Say About Alpha.* Alpha News, November 1996.

Alpha. *Papal Preacher gives Alpha Follow-Up Talks.* Alpha News, July – October 1999.

Andrews, Cecil. *The Toronto 'Blessing' Is No Laughing Matter.* 'Take Heed' Publications, 1995.

Andrews, Cecil. *An Alpha Assessment: Nicky Gumbel's 'Gospel'.* 'News From The Front': 'Take Heed' Ministries, December 2000.

Bagnall, Leila. *They floated away.* Alpha News, July – October 2003.

Chapman, Tim. *The Alpha Course Examined.* The Theologian website, 2002: <http://www.geocities.com/the_theologian/content/pastoralia/alpha.html>.

Correspondent. *Alpha and Papacy Move Closer.* British Church Newspaper, 9 January 2004.

Correspondent. *6-Day creation 'rubbish' says Steve Chalke.* British Church Newspaper, 20 August 2004.

Fitch, Thomas. *Straight Talks.* Marshall, Morgan & Scott Ltd., 1950.

Gallagher, Gerard. *A Way To Grow The Church.* The Irish Catholic, 10 September 1998.

Gumbel, Nicky. *The Spirit and Evangelism.* Renewal, May 1995 as quoted by Elizabeth McDonald in *Alpha: New Life or New Lifestyle?*

Guthrie, Donald. *The Pastoral Epistles.* Inter-Varsity Press, 1996.

Hand, Chris. *Falling Short: The Alpha Course Examined.* Day One Publications, 1998.

Hand, Chris. *Alpha Holy Spirit Weekend Claims Celebrity Casualty.* CRN News No 9, 2000.

Henry, Matthew. *Commentary on the Whole Bible: Volume V.* Fleming H Revell Company, 1935.

Jordan, Diane Louise. *This is the best thing that has ever happened to me.* Alpha News, March – July 2000.

Mackay, Norman. *A False Sense of Security.* Evangelical Times, August 2002.

Morrison, Alan. *How the Toronto 'Blessing' Came to Town.* Evangelical Times, November 1994.

McCullough, Raymond. *Alpha Conference Dublin.* Bread Magazine: Vol. 4: No. 3, March/April/May 1996.

McDonald, Elizabeth. *Alpha: New Life or New Lifestyle?* St Matthew Publishing Ltd., 1996.

Ostling, Richard N. *Laughing For The Lord.* Time Magazine, 15 August 1994.

Panosian, Edward. *The World Council of Churches.* Bob Jones University Press, 1983.

Pink, Arthur W. *The Attributes of God.* Baker Book House, 1980.

Richardson, Neil. *Nicky Gumbel and the Alpha Course.* Christian Witness Ministries, 2000.

Ryan, Sam. *I was into crystal healing.* Alpha News, March – June 2003.

Ryle, J C. *Expository Thoughts on Matthew.* The Banner of Truth Trust, 1986.

Spurgeon, Charles H. *2200 Quotations from the Writings of Charles H. Spurgeon.* Tom Carter (compiler). Baker Books, 1996.

Thomas, Geoff. *Is This Revival?* Evangelical Times, September 1994.

Thomas, Geoff. *William Barclay and The Plain Man.* Evangelical Times, January 1997.

Thompson, Damian. *Charisma Comes To Kensington.* Daily Telegraph, 22 December 1990.

Zenit News. *Papal Household Preacher Reflects on The Trinity.* Zenit Daily Bulletin: Vatican City, 17 June 2003.

Printed in the United Kingdom
by Lightning Source UK Ltd.
102025UKS00001B/97-183